# *CROSSCHECK*
## NORTHBROOK HOCKEY ELITE

Rebecca Connolly
Heather B. Moore
Sophia Summers

# *CROSSCHECK*
## NORTHBROOK HOCKEY ELITE

Copyright © 2020 by Rebecca Connolly
Print edition
All rights reserved

No part of this book may be reproduced in any form whatsoever without prior written permission of the publisher, except in the case of brief passages embodied in critical reviews and articles. This is a work of fiction. The characters, names, incidents, places, and dialog are products of the author's imagination and are not to be construed as real.

Interior design by Cora Johnson
Edited by Kelsey Down and Lorie Humpherys
Cover design by Rachael Anderson
Cover image credit: Deposit Photos #46575443
Published by Mirror Press, LLC

ISBN: 978-1-947152-94-6

## NORTHBROOK HOCKEY ELITE SERIES

Faceoff
Powerplay
Rebound
Crosscheck
Breakaway
Shootout

## Dedication

To the Chicago Blackhawks, who have created a lifelong fan in me and shown me just how amazing this sport is. I can honestly say that I wouldn't have been able to do this series without you. And thank you seems much too small.

And to my uncle Pete. Your strength, humor, goodness, and generosity have never impressed me more than they do now. Love you forever.

# CROSSCHECK

He's a hard hitter, she's a straight shooter. Can they stop the sparks from flying? Do they want to?

Zane Winchester is a beast on the ice, known for racking up penalties and delivering hard blows. No one would suspect the complicated nature of his personal life, or just what it entailed. And no one, not even him, would have suspected what one unexpected encounter with a remarkable woman would do to his life.

Mara Matthews is a regular woman with a regular job and a regular life. Then she meets the father of one of her little students, and regular becomes the last word to describe her life. Zane is intense, funny, charming, and drop dead gorgeous; he shouldn't pay any attention to someone like her. But Zane isn't giving up, and Mara doesn't want him to.

# ONE

"High-sticking, two minutes."

"WHAT?"

The referee gave Zane Winchester a knowing look. "Come on, Zamboni, head to the box."

Zane debated taking a stance on the ice, towering over the ref as he was, but he opted, probably wisely, for skating backwards towards his very cozy and well-loved penalty box. "So about that call . . ."

"Zamboni, you know better than to argue a penalty."

"I'm not arguing it," he insisted with a good-natured smile. "I know I deserve it. Just not for high-sticking. That was a hook, Jim. Come on. I never go for the shoulders."

The ref rolled his eyes and gestured to the box, then signaled to the staff working the clock, who put two minutes up on the jumbotron.

Zane shrugged and stepped into the box, sitting down and making a show of stretching out, earning some laughter and applause from the fans behind the plexiglass at the back of the box. He turned and waved at them, then returned his attention to the game.

Not that he needed to pay attention.

The Hounds, his team, were already up by two goals in the third period, and it would have been more had they been really focusing. They had been for the first two periods, but now...

Well, Zane had resorted to intentionally delivering penalties to see what would get caught.

Now he'd been caught for the wrong one.

Figured.

But he was famous for his rough hitting and his collection of penalties, which had been his trademark since the age of fourteen.

Maybe younger...

It was hard to remember when he had earned his nickname, Zamboni, but he did remember the Northbrook Elite teammates that had been in hysterics as they explained, "Because you just clear the ice!"

He'd loved the name from that moment. It had been one of the first times he'd felt the approval of his teammates rather than their mockery.

Zane had been a late bloomer.

'Nuff said.

Looking down the ice, Zane whistled to himself, thumping the butt of his stick against the floor of the box in time with whatever tune he was performing.

The penalty box was designed to be a time-out for the offending players, disciplinary action that was supposed to give them a chance to think about what they did wrong and how it was affecting others.

Zane always thought it was a nice breather away from the rest of the team.

He liked them well enough, but the penalty box gave him way more shoulder room.

What would happen if he pretended to meditate in here? He could sit perfectly still, eyes closed, completely at peace, unaffected by the sounds of the game and its fans around him. Then, when the time was up, he could spring out of the penalty box like a shot, invigorated and full of harnessed hatred.

It would be a glorious act.

He grinned slowly to himself. He'd save that one for another time. There were only a few seconds left in this particular penalty, and then he'd go out and hit some unsuspecting Florida Jaguar players.

Or maybe they would suspect it. He was fairly infamous, after all.

He'd hate to disappoint anyone.

Zane eyed the crowd in the stands, grunting to himself that some of the local fans were leaving already. He couldn't blame them, given the score and the time left, but the game wasn't over. Would it kill them to stick it out?

A flash of brilliant green amidst the sea of black and gold caught his attention, and he jerked back to look at it more closely.

The Jaguars were blue and white; there was no cause for anything green to be here.

With perfect timing, the green banner was spread out to its full length, with the help of the fans bearing it.

*Sabercats.*

The Northbrook mascot.

Zane grinned and got to his feet, pointing to the classiest fans in this entire arena, whooping at the top of his lungs. They began to jump up and down, the banner rippling like a wave.

He glanced up at the clock, watching as the last few seconds ticked down, then burst from the box with a jolt of speed. His eyes darted around the ice, then he made a beeline for a winger making life complicated for the Hounds' center. Zane clocked him hard but perfectly legally, sending him flying into the boards.

The crowd erupted, as they usually did when the Zamboni did something without getting called for it.

Zane watched his teammates take the puck down the ice, flicking it between themselves, then sending it soaring into the net just between the legs of the goalie before his knees hit the ice.

The piercing sound of the buzzer rang throughout the arena, and Zane pumped his arms in the air in victory as the crowd stomped their approval. He turned to find the Northbrook group again and directed his cheering towards them once more.

He didn't recognize a single one of them.

It didn't matter; Northbrook was on its second wind these days, coming back from the dead almost literally with a vibrant new fan base and an increased loyalty from the alumni.

He might be a Hound now, but he was first, foremost, and forevermore a Sabercat.

He wasn't used to that kind of loyalty. He'd felt it while he was there, for sure, but when he'd left, his loyalty had been to himself and whatever team he currently played for. That was all.

Now . . .

Well, he couldn't exactly say he had matured, but he was certainly wiser than he had once been.

When he felt like it.

At the signal from his coach, Zane skated to the team box and slipped over the edge of it with ease. He plopped himself down on the bench and caught a water bottle from one of the assistants one-handed, guzzling it almost in the same motion.

"Show-off."

Zane paused his hydration process to give the guy next to him a sidelong look.

Petey wasn't intimidated, and he raised a brow, daring Zane to give him a comeback of some kind.

Squeezing the bottle again, Zane took another three gulps before exhaling heavily and tossing it back without really looking. "Skills, Petey. Not seeking attention."

"No," Petey drawled, his northern Minnesota accent proudly ringing through. "Why would you do that? You hate attention."

"I do. I'm really very shy." Zane nodded, which sent chuckles down the line of guys.

"Terribly insecure," Janny added from his left, barely displaying any of his Swedish roots in saying so. "Poor Zamboni."

"Poor Zamboni," several voices echoed with solemnity.

Zane looked up and down the line, smiling quizzically. "Did I die somewhere along the way? This is a crap memorial service, if I did."

Two guys removed their helmets and bowed their heads, sending the rest into roars of laughter.

"Unbelievable," Zane muttered, shaking his head.

"Hey, hey!" Coach Winkler hollered at them all. "Three minutes left in this game. Don't start monkeying around!"

Zane turned his attention forward with the rest, all shutting up without another word. Wink was a tough coach, and despite their good record so far this season, he still acted like this was the team from five years ago that almost never won. He was right, in this instance; they should continue to pay attention to the game, support their teammates, and keep their focus on the ice.

There ought to be a level of respect for the other team as well, no matter how badly they were being beaten.

"Kelso line, go!" Wink bellowed suddenly.

Zane frowned but cheered the three guys onto the ice as they currently line skated off towards them. What was Wink expecting the Kelso line to do with two and a half minutes left when they were already up by three? There was nothing to be gained by scoring again, and Kelso was a maniac.

Coming from Zane, that was a pretty damning description.

Kelso scooped up the puck and took it around the back of their own goal, cradling it from side to side with his stick, sending it to Petey on his left to get around a player before it was back to him. He swept right, then left, deking with incredible speed, completely ignoring Ramsey on his right side, despite Ramsey's calling for the puck.

What was that about?

The Jaguar defenders were on Kelso then, and he scuffled neatly, somehow avoiding giving up the puck despite the clashing of blades and sticks.

"Get it out!" Zane bellowed, getting to his feet with some of the teammates. "Clear it!"

Kelso kept the puck, for some insane reason, and a third Jaguar player was headed in their direction. There would be nothing to do at that point but wait for the puck to clear towards the Hound goal rather than in the direction they wanted.

"NOW!" Petey bellowed.

With inhuman accuracy, Kelso delivered a slapshot no one could touch, not towards the goal but towards Ramsey, who had continued down the ice without anyone paying much attention. Ramsey scooped the puck and shot it at the goal, right in a tight corner the goalie hadn't a hope of covering with the distraction of Kelso's antics.

The Hounds' box exploded with cheers and laughter,

teammates calling out words of praise and appreciation, if not outright razzing. The score didn't matter, and none of them cared about the numbers on that board with regards to the win.

That play had been a beautiful thing. Insane, reckless, risky, and completely out of control, but a beautiful thing.

Kelso was a hotshot, a twenty-year-old kid who almost owned the ice once he touched it. Zane had never seen anything like him, which was saying something.

Unfortunately, Kelso also had the attitude to go with it.

Zane had been inches away from pounding him on more than one occasion during practice.

There was a quick faceoff after the goal, and the puck flitted harmlessly across the ice between players until the clock ran out and the buzzer sounded.

The Hounds came out of their team box onto the ice to shake hands with the Jaguars, none of whom looked particularly happy. Zane and his teammates turned their attention to the crowd and their fans, trying to pump up whoever was left in the stands in gratitude for giving them so much energy during the course of the game.

As usual, he was one of the last ones out there.

Zane might not be captain material, and likely never would be, but no one could accuse him of not caring about the fans.

He exhaled roughly as he left the ice, making his way towards the locker rooms. He tugged his helmet off and ran a hand through his drenched hair, sending droplets everywhere. He craned his neck, eliciting a series of cracks on one side, then the other. Away from the ice and the energy of the fans, Zane could admit something he almost never did aloud: he was exhausted. Physically and mentally exhausted.

They'd done a home-and-home series with the Ravens—

one game in Tennessee followed by one the next night in Seattle—then had just one night off before tonight's game, thankfully at home. Before the Ravens, they'd had three away games in a week, and he'd been up in Chicago with some of his old Northbrook guys doing an all-star game.

He'd barely sat down since the holidays, it seemed, and he wanted nothing more right now than to sleep for about five days.

But if anybody asked, he was in the best shape of his life, top of his game, full of energy, and wanting extra games and practices to stay sharp.

No one had ever told Zane that by the age of twenty-eight he would feel so old.

He sat down at his locker, stripping off his uniform and pads, taking care not to inhale too deeply.

The stench of his gear had never been something he'd wanted to have lingering about his nostrils and lungs.

He wanted to live to see twenty-nine.

Hiding a yawn behind a hand and stretching, he headed into the showers, slapping hands with a few already departing teammates.

He may have stood in the shower for a very long time, just letting the hot water rain down on him, but once he'd come to his senses and realized what time it was, he scrubbed his hair and body as fast as sanitarily possible. He changed his clothes, set his gear in the laundry cart, and headed out at a fast clip.

The drive home was uneventful, as it usually was at this time of night. His teammates had sent around the usual texts about going out for drinks and food, and some of them for less-than-savory entertainment, but Zane ignored them all. No one would be upset by that, as he usually did the same after every game and most practices.

He had other things to do.

Better things.

He was all for spending time with his teammates, team building and whatever else their coaches and sport psychologists encouraged among them.

Just not this late.

He glanced at the clock on his dashboard, hissing softly and risking going just a little further above the speed limit than he might normally do.

His neighbor was a cop; surely if the worst happened, he could be let off . . .

Zane released a breath he hadn't known he'd been holding as he pulled into his neighborhood and, just a few minutes later, into the driveway. Glancing up into the windows on the opposite side from the garage, he hissed again when he saw only the very faintest of light there.

He was in trouble now.

"Hey, Zane!"

He turned in surprise to see Steve, his cop neighbor, hauling the trash cans down his own driveway, wearing an oversized Hounds sweatshirt from days gone by and a black beanie on his head, despite the fact that the Tennessee night was a mild forty-two degrees.

Zane smiled with a wave. "Steve."

"Good game," his neighbor called, a proud Tennessee twang ringing out.

"Thanks, man." He pointed at his house. "Sorry, I gotta get. I'm late."

Steve chuckled and waved him on. "Go ahead, buddy. She's been on one today. You're in for it."

Zane grunted and continued for the house. "Don't I know it. Thanks, Steve."

"Leave your garage open, Zane. I'll get your trash out."

Zane turned back around in surprise. "You don't have to do that."

Steve only shrugged. "I know. Go on in there and take your punishment. I got this."

Zane shook his head and pointed. "You're a good man, Steve."

"Yep, well, put a word in with the Lord for me, cuz no one else will."

It was one of the more Southern expressions Zane had heard, and he chuckled as he made his way into the house.

He dropped his keys on the counter and his bag on the floor, not stopping his motion towards the stairs.

A tousled head rose from the couch on the other side of the stairs, eyes squinting in his direction. "Zane?"

He smiled and waved her back down, swinging himself up the stairs by the railing. "Go back to sleep, Josie. Better yet, go to bed, I'm back."

His cousin yawned without shame, rubbing at one eye. "You're in trouble, you know."

"Gee, thanks," he muttered as he took the stairs two at a time.

He walked cautiously once he reached the second floor, wincing when the floorboards creaked beneath him. Served him right for buying a classic house instead of a new construction, but his realtor had assured him it would be much better on resale.

Whatever.

He reached the door and hesitated, craning his neck again but this time without the satisfying cracks.

He hated being in trouble.

Gripping the doorknob, he gently turned it, easing the door open, the night-light in the corner the only light he could see by. A small fan was going on the nightstand, making any sound within the room harder to hear.

He waited, straining his ears.

"You said before bedtime."

Zane exhaled noisily and pushed into the room fully, dropping to his knees beside the small twin bed, smoothing the bow-patterned comforter out of habit. "I know, pumpkin. I'm sorry, the game went late."

"Did you win?"

The question came on a very young yawn, and he smiled at it, looking into the face of his daughter with a fond smile. "Of course."

Hope smiled at him, her one vacant tooth leaving an adorable gap in her otherwise perfect smile. "Josie let me watch part of the game tonight."

Zane pretended to be put out. "Did she? Which part did you see?"

"The part where you got tripped. Did you get hurt?"

Good, she'd seen the beginning of the game, then. That had been a safe enough portion. "No, Hopey, Daddy didn't get hurt. I'm fine, see?" He flexed his arm while growling.

Hope was unimpressed. "We have to study the letter $N$ tomorrow. You don't have a game, right?"

"Nope, so we can study the letter $N$ all you want. I love the letter $N$. Noodles, night-lights, naps . . . nnwaffles . . ."

Now his daughter giggled and playfully slapped his arm. "That's not a word, silly."

Zane gasped. "It's not? Guess I better study hard with you, huh?"

Hope yawned again, and Zane leaned closer, brushing her thick, dark curls away from her brow. "Daddy?"

"Hmm?"

"How many days until my birthday?"

He smiled at the nightly question's appearance. "What is today's date?"

She counted carefully. "Second."

"Good. So how many days? Count it out."

She tried, she really did, but then she huffed and looked at him. "I need your hands too."

He offered both hands while she counted out on them.

When she ran out of fingers, she counted his eyes and nose as well. "Twenty-three!" she cried.

"Very good. That's my smart girl." He smiled proudly and stroked her hair again. "You ready to go to sleep now?"

She nodded and nestled into her pillow. "I'm ready."

"Sleep says the daddy-o," he recited, his thumb smoothing over her brow. "Sleep says the light. Sleep says the teddy bear . . ."

Hope snuggled her teddy close and sighed, "And Hopey says, 'Night-night, night.'"

Zane nodded and pushed up a little, pressing a soft kiss to his baby girl's forehead. "Good night, baby. I love you."

"I love you too, Daddy," she replied, smiling before she shut her eyes and turned her head away.

He stayed there for a moment, still on his knees, watching Hope as she relaxed further into her bed.

How much longer would she want him to come see her before she went to bed? How many more times would he recite their nightly rhyme, either by her bedside or over the phone?

How long would she remain his baby girl?

He didn't want to think about it, couldn't bear the thought of anything changing. Not after everything else that had changed in their lives.

Shaking his head, he got to his feet and exited her room, softly shutting her door behind him.

No matter what any of his teammates thought was the perfect way to end a night with a win, it could not compete with this.

Not even close.

# TWO

Sweat poured down her overheated face. Her heart pounded against her chest with almost painful fury. Air wasn't coming or going easily. Her legs and arms burned in agony, begging her to stop.

It was almost over now.

Almost . . .

"And march it out!" Mara Matthews grinned out at her class, all following her instructions to the best of their abilities. "Who's tired? Anyone?"

"No!" a chorus of voices called, some of them giggling together after bellowing their response.

Mara gaped out at them. "You're *not*? I'm exhausted! I don't think we can do one more song, can we?"

"Yes!" the children called, responses much less together this time, as some of the girls repeated their answer multiple times for emphasis.

Mara wiped a hand over her brow in pretend fatigue. "Okay, I guess we can try just one more . . ." She nodded at her class assistant, who knew exactly which song to play.

The moment the beginning notes sounded, the kids cheered.

She knew they'd have that reaction; the three previous classes that morning had done the exact same thing, and considering it was a hit from one of the most popular children's movies of the winter, she suspected it would be playing in her class for some time.

Mara didn't mind. Good music for kids was actually pretty difficult. Movie soundtracks were pretty much all she had, but she didn't mind.

She loved movie soundtracks for kids.

She saw most of those movies herself.

Might have indulged in some car-based karaoke with some of her own favorites.

She'd never tell.

"All right, hands above the head and clap!" she called, demonstrating the clapping to the beat of the song. "Clap! Clap! Clap! Now stomp, two, three, four . . ."

She continued on in her cheeriest voice, most of the kids able to follow the instructions well enough. Coordination wasn't required for her classes, only enthusiasm, and they were very good with the enthusiasm.

"And turn, two, three, four," Mara instructed, enjoying the giggles that erupted when the girls couldn't manage to turn and move sideways at the same time. "Forward, two, three, four, to the left . . ."

Two little girls in the back, who were identical in appearance except for the fact that they looked nothing alike, screeched in hilarity as they crashed into each other. They were dressed in perfect coordination with each other, down to the laces on their shoes and the height of their pigtails. Their blue skirts over pink leggings made Mara smile, and she made a mental note to host a princess day sometime soon for her class.

She had a decent ball gown that she'd be able to instruct in well enough.

Maybe not breathe, but instructing should be fine.

"Clap again!" she told the class. "And step and clap, left, right, left, right . . ."

She had to laugh as the kids tried to roll their arms from side to side as she did, a few in the back managing well enough, while the little ones couldn't seem to figure it out.

It didn't keep them from enjoying themselves. Did nothing to remove the smiles from their faces.

That was one of the things she loved best about teaching the kids' classes. Their limitations did not affect their enjoyment. There was no pride to block their way, no fear of judgment, and no hesitation in giving each song everything they had.

Mara would teach exercise classes for kids a dozen times a day rather than teach one adult class.

Since no one else at the club had any interest in any of the kids' classes, she didn't have to worry about that. After all, these classes had been her idea.

Well, they'd been her niece's idea, technically, after Mara had grown particularly desperate for entertainment options when Maddie's mom and dad had taken longer than expected to come home. Four songs from a movie later, and both little girls had stopped fighting, being reduced to breathless giggling instead.

"You should make an exercise class like this, Aunt Mara," her niece had said. "That was so much fun, and good for us too, right?"

And here she was, every Saturday morning now spoken for, sleeping in reduced to only one day a week.

Such was the sacrifice.

"Big finale!" She put her hands on her hips. "And jump and shimmy. Jump and shimmy. Jump and body roll!"

Giggles rent the air, and hers were among them.

That was another reason she didn't mind the sacrifice; their joy was infectious.

"Big roll of the arms down low," she called. "Roll it all the way up . . . and punch, punch, punch, WOO!"

The kids echoed her cheer, tiny fists lifted in the air, some still giggling while they did so.

Mara smiled widely and clapped. "There we go! That was great; you guys are getting so good! We are all done for today."

Groans and whining rose up from the group, and Mara pouted for effect.

"I know, guys, I know! But it's okay, we'll see you back here next week! And do you remember what next Saturday is?"

The would-be twins in the back raised their hands.

Mara grinned and pointed at them. "Hope and Claire?"

"Kids' choice!" they cried.

"That's right! Find your favorite songs to dance to, and we just might get to do that next time!"

That seemed to get rid of the disappointment, and all of the kids chattered about what they might pick as they moved to the back of the room to get their bags and bottles of water.

"Okay, kids," the room assistant called, "don't forget, you can leave this room, but you have to stay on this side of the rainbow desk until your parent comes and signs you out!"

None of the kids were particularly listening, but they knew the rule well. It wasn't often that they wanted to go past the rainbow desk anyway, considering Miss Hannah always had treats there for the ones who were patient. Sometimes healthy treats, sometimes not, but always there were treats.

And Miss Hannah didn't have any problem with refusing to hand it out if someone broke the rules.

Mara exhaled roughly as the kids began to trickle out of the room to see what Miss Hannah had on hand today. She wiped at her brow, this time not faking it, and sat on the floor with a groan, stretching her legs out and bending at the waist over them, wishing she could actually get her nose to touch the black leggings she wore like she'd once been able to. With adulthood had come a decrease in her flexibility, and try as she might, she couldn't bring it back.

"I don't know how you do it."

Mara straightened and gave a tired smile to the room assistant, who was not her usual one and whose name she had completely forgotten from earlier in the morning. "Do what?"

"Teach four of those classes in a row!" The woman shook her head, tight black braids swinging back and forth. "Girl, you've got more energy than half of those kids, and the patience of a saint."

"No, I really don't," Mara insisted with a laugh. "I'm really good at faking it, and I plan on a serious nap when I get home. If I can move."

The assistant wrinkled her nose, making a face as Mara stretched her legs out to the side and groaned. "Sore today?"

Mara nodded. "I didn't sleep well, woke up so tight, and then the classes . . ." She laughed again and squinted up at the woman. "Getting moving was a whole lot easier when I was a teenager."

That earned her a snort of derision. "Honey, wait until forty comes around. Nothing moves the way it should, and other things move that never moved before." She shook her head, frowning dramatically. "Mmm. Just ain't right." Whistling for effect, the assistant shook her head one more time as she walked towards the doors of the room, picking up a few towels that had been left behind by students.

Mara chuckled and bent herself at the waist again, reaching her hands out, crawling her fingers forward along the floor. She hissed and sighed when she reached her limits, and she put her head down, relaxing her shoulders until her arms seemed to just land alongside her.

She hadn't exaggerated to the assistant; she really had slept poorly—kinked her back or some such—and moving today hadn't been nearly as easy as it should have been. She wasn't the most limber person in the world, but she definitely didn't have spasms in her back from four Zumba classes for kids most of the time. She bent her knees and brought her legs to center, rising up just enough to pull her legs beneath her until she was curled into a ball. She exhaled slowly, then rocked her hips back until she felt her shoes on her behind before walking her hands forward again.

This time she groaned at the perfect stretch in her particularly sore back. Biting down on her lip, she forced herself to breathe more deeply, trying to get her coiled muscles to relax.

The soreness radiating in her arms and legs told her that wasn't particularly likely today.

Oh well.

"What are you doing?"

Mara froze in the middle of her lame attempt at relaxation breathing, and she lifted her head.

One of the almost twins stood there, looking strangely small without her counterpart, brown pigtails lopsided due to the tilt of her head, quizzical expression on her adorable face.

Was this one Hope or Claire? One was a redhead, the other brunette, but they were so close and united in everything, telling them apart was a challenge.

"This," Mara informed the girl, frantically trying to figure out her name while smiling at her, "is called Child's Pose. And it's helping me stretch out, which is important to do after exercise."

"My daddy is *always* stretching," the girl said with a

dramatic roll of her eyes. Then she frowned. "Miss Mara, why didn't we stretch after class if it's important?"

This was a smart one, and Mara doubted she missed much.

She liked her more for that.

"We ran out of time," Mara told her apologetically.

"Can I stretch with you now?"

Mara nodded and gestured beside her. "Of course. See how my legs are?"

The little girl nodded and came to sit on her heels next to Mara, her tongue sticking out a little as she adjusted her position in an attempt to mirror her. She stretched her arms out as far as she could go, strain evident on her face, her bum high in the air rather than at her heels. "Like this?"

"Almost," Mara replied, trying desperately not to laugh. "Try to touch your bum to your shoes. See?" She wiggled her feet to show them off.

"Oh." A frown appeared on the young face, and she forced herself back before trying to stretch her hands out again.

Mara nodded with a smile. "There you go. That's it, don't lift off, just stay there. Good!"

"I feel it!" The little girl grinned over at her with pride. "Am I stretching?"

"You are!" Mara lowered her head to continue her own stretch. "Lower your head a little. Feel that in your neck?"

"Yeah! Let's do another one!"

Mara chuckled. "Hold on, we need a few more seconds. Can you count to fifteen for us?"

She did so, drawing each number out as though she were about to start hide and seek.

"Good. Now we're going to sit up . . ." She moved into position, waiting for her stretching partner to do the same.

"And then reach one arm over your head and lean to the same side."

They both did so, Mara wincing at the tension flaring in her back at the action while her tiny partner seemed more focused than anyone should be while stretching.

"Fifteen!" called the girl. "And switch!"

Mara laughed out loud and did so, giving her a look. "You were very good at that. Are you trying to take my job?"

"No!"

"You sure?"

"Hopey-Dopey, where are you?"

Mara looked up at the door of the room to see a thin, beautiful woman in perfectly fitted workout clothes standing there, grinning at the little girl, perspiring in a way that Mara could only describe as glistening.

She'd never glistened in her entire life.

Red-faced and dripping was more Mara's style.

Embarrassing wet patches on workout tanks.

Random strands of hair rising from her scalp and curling at odd angles.

That was Mara.

Not this perfection embodied, who apparently had just gotten enough of a workout to feel satisfied while looking as though she were modeling the workout clothes rather than functioning in them.

But that didn't matter right now. Not really.

Mara looked at the girl beside her, who was, it seemed, Hope and not Claire.

"We're stretching!" Hope cheerily called with a wave. "It's important after exercise."

"I know," the woman replied. "I just finished my stretching."

Faintly Mara wondered if *she* was able to touch her nose to her kneecaps.

Perfection tossed her long, perfectly blond ponytail and gave another dazzling smile. "I'm sorry, bug, but we really do need to go. Remember why?"

Hope gasped almost dramatically. "Ooh! I forgot!" She jumped up and dashed to the door but turned around before she reached it. "Thank you for the class, Miss Mara, and thank you for stretching with me."

Mara folded her legs in and smiled at her. "You are very welcome, Hope. See you next week."

Hope waved and dashed out of the room, Perfection following behind her.

So not fair.

Sighing, Mara got to her feet and made her way out of the room, flipping off the lights as she did so. Out at the rainbow desk, Miss Hannah was giving out the last of the treats to the few straggling kids.

"All done, Mara?" Miss Hannah asked without looking up. "You must be tired."

Mara smiled at her and took the baggie of cookies from the basket when it was offered. "I am, but these will help."

"And you worked all week?"

"Of course. Dr. Hayden is as busy as ever, and I'm busy running his schedule. After that madness?" She gestured to the giggling kids waiting to be picked up. "This is easy."

Miss Hannah laughed and waved as one of the little girls left the children's section with her mother. "If you say so. Oh dear." Miss Hannah came around the edge of the desk and picked up a pink jacket. "I think Hope left this behind."

It was too chilly outside this morning for anyone to go without a coat of some kind, and Mara hated to think of that little sweetheart getting a cold in her excitement to go.

"I'll run it out to her," Mara offered, holding out her hand for the coat. "They can't have gone far."

Miss Hannah gave it to her, and Mara hurried out of the children's section into the rest of the gym. Her steps were quick as she darted around the machines and guests, smiling at the trainers working with their clients, and made her way to the front of the building.

Hope still held the hand of the perfect blond, who had to be her mother, though how any woman went from having a baby to having that body was unfathomable. They didn't look that much alike, but Hope probably took after her dad.

What kind of guy managed to get Perfection to fall for him?

"Hope!" Mara called, trying to drag herself out of her jealous thoughts. "Hope!"

They didn't hear her, and she hustled more, jogging now.

The windows at the front of the gym took up almost the entire wall, and just as she reached the doors, she saw Hope through those windows, running into the arms of a mountain of a man with the most perfect shoulders she'd ever seen encased in a fleece jacket. The man wore a baseball cap and sunglasses, despite the fact that it was an overcast morning and chilly. Normally, Mara would have hated something like that, but this guy . . .

She swallowed as the unzipped fleece, combined with his exuberant actions with the little girl, revealed a tight T-shirt that hid absolutely nothing about his abs.

Perfect abs.

The sort of abs Perfection would totally go for.

Gulp.

She watched for a moment as Hope showed off some of the dance moves they had done in class today, her dark-haired, mysterious father giving her every bit of attention she deserved, clapping and praising her as though she were on a stage somewhere. He pretended to be very impressed, which made Mara smile where she stood.

Then he held out a hand, which Hope took at once, and they started towards the cars.

Right. Jacket.

Mara pushed out of the doors, swallowing a sudden awkward lump. "Hope! Hope, wait!"

The family turned in surprise, and Mara forced a bright smile, the cold air suddenly much colder in her sweat-dampened state.

Which meant her hair would be dirty and frizzy, her face red, and her armpits sweaty.

Oh good. This was how she was going to meet Hope's hunky dad?

No way.

She waved the jacket. "Silly goose, you left this inside. It's way too cold out here, you need it!"

As she'd figured, Hope dashed over to her, leaving the others and stopping right in front of her.

"We had to go meet Daddy," Hope explained as she put the jacket on. "We're going out to lunch!"

"You lucky girl!" Mara smiled and helped zip her up. "Just make sure you keep the jacket on outside, okay? You need to stay warm. Deal?"

"Deal!" Hope flashed a quick grin, then ran back to her family.

Mara nodded, at no one in particular, and turned to go back into the gym, hoping no one would see the sweat stains she could feel on her back.

"Daddy, that's my teacher, Miss Mara. Don't you think she's so pretty?"

A choking sensation gripped Mara even as her ears strained to hear the answer.

Her feet, however, kept moving, and faster than they should have been.

Married fathers of students, and their opinions on her looks, were no business of hers.

None at all.

Not that it made any difference, as Hope's dad had the good sense to lower his voice enough that she didn't even hear him say anything at all.

The warm gust of air that hit her as she went back into the gym was welcome, but it did nothing for the heat in her cheeks or the tension in her chest.

"Hoo," she said on a rough exhale, sniffing and shaking her head.

That was quite enough of that.

"Hey, Mara!" came the booming voice of Ray, one of the gym's trainers. "Wanna come do a few sets? I have some free time."

Mara shook her head quickly but smiled for him. "Thanks, Ray, but I'm beat. I'm gonna go home. There's a pint of ice cream there with my name on it, and I really, really need it."

# THREE

ANXIETY WASN'T SOMETHING that Zane was particularly accustomed to, but at this moment, he saw danger everywhere.

He hated malls.

He hated everything about them.

His baseball cap could only hide so much, and there was no way he could get away with wearing sunglasses indoors. Not while he was shopping with Hope. That wouldn't be a disguise; it would be a signal to the mall cops to swarm him for kidnapping.

Nothing like standing out when you wanted to blend in, really. Not that blending in was exactly easy in his case. But it wasn't his fault he was six foot six and weighing in at two hundred and twenty-two pounds, as this morning's scale had informed him. That was all due to genetics, training, and a blessing by the hockey gods.

Thankfully, Tennessee was full of people of all sizes, and nobody really looked at his face when he walked around. Nobody really looked at anybody's faces. For the number of famous people walking around Nashville, people really did seem to mind their own business for the most part.

And Zane Winchester wasn't exactly the most famous person in Nashville.

He wasn't even the most famous athlete in Nashville.

Not when Chezzy was dating the next-hottest gal on the country music stage and the college basketball season was ramping up towards its finale. Nobody was as famous as the music stars around here, and he had never met a more passionate fan base than the college fans.

They came out in full force for the Hounds, it was true, but seeing the players without their helmets on was rare, and fans could never be quite sure about identities.

He cupped his hand around the well-molded bill of his cap almost out of habit, trying to hide his features further by its shadow.

If he were out in this madness by himself, he wouldn't care so much.

But he wasn't alone.

"Daddy!"

He looked down at his little princess, her hand in his, her hot-pink fleece not doing anything to make her blend in. "Hopey?"

She gave him the sort of look only teenagers should wear. "You said we could go to the stuffed animal store. The one where I can make my own."

Zane gave her a crooked grin, shaking the hand he held so that the motion would ripple across her whole arm. "I said no such thing, pumpkin. I said *for your birthday*, if you wanted, we could go. It would be one of your presents."

Hope narrowed her dark eyes up at him, suspicion etched in every feature.

It was adorable on her.

It was exactly the way her mother had looked at times.

Which had not been adorable.

At all.

"I don't think that's what you said," his daughter said moodily.

"I think I did," Zane assured her. "I promise."

Hope seemed to think about that for a moment. Then she brightened. "How will I know if I want to go there for my birthday if I've never even been inside of it?"

She had him there.

Zane scowled. "That's a dirty trick, kid."

"So we can go?" She beamed hopefully up at him.

She already knew she'd won.

So did he.

"Fine," he grumbled. "But dinner first, okay?"

"Food court dinner?" Hope shot back.

This time there was no argument from Zane. "Of course. Know what you want?"

"Cheeseburger!" she cried with all the enthusiasm a five-year-old girl could conjure up.

Zane chuckled and shook his head. "That's my girl. Okay, let's go see what our cheeseburger options are."

The food court was packed, as he had expected, but the options were straightforward enough. Italian, Japanese, pizza, sandwich place, healthy place, smoothie place, two burger places, and something European he couldn't quite decide if he was brave enough to try. If it were up to him, he'd go to the more classic burger place: more like bar food than fast food, and the portions more his style.

But his five-year-old was in charge, and she wanted fast food.

The kids meals came with toys.

There was no arguing with that.

Sighing, Zane got into line with all of the other people, Hope's attention fixed on the display of possible toys for her meal. "Daddy, I hope the green princess is the one we get. Lookit, she flies! You just pull the string on her flower, and she takes off!"

"How about that?" he replied automatically, scanning the menu for them both.

"No! I want the purple one!" Hope gasped, squeezing his hand as she jumped up and down. "Daddy, she comes with makeup!"

He blinked, his focus on the menu broken momentarily. "She has what now?"

"Look!"

He followed the direction of Hope's finger, suddenly determined that nothing of the sort was coming home with his baby girl. She was growing up as it was, and to have makeup as a side dish to her meal? No way, no how.

"Don't worry," a man standing nearby with two girls of his own muttered. "My girls asked, and they don't have any purple ones tonight."

Zane didn't bother hiding his relief and nodded his thanks to a fellow father in distress. "Thanks, man. What are they thinking with that sort of thing?"

His new ally whistled low. "I don't want to know, brother. Good luck."

Zane nodded again, smiling to himself as they moved up the line. "Which other ones do you like, Hope?"

She rattled off the fun things about the other four fairies, proving his fear that she was paying more attention to TV commercials than he would have liked, right up until they were at the counter themselves.

"Hi there, what can I get for y'all this evening?" their chipper, high-school-aged cashier asked.

Zane looked down at Hope. "What do you want, pumpkin?"

Hope eyed the cashier, then hugged herself close to Zane, burying her face against his side.

"Go on," he encouraged gently, one hand going to her hair and stroking softly.

She shook her head against him.

He sighed to himself at that. Hope had developed this shyness with strangers lately, and he wasn't sure why. She'd been a tough nut to crack as a toddler, only waving or smiling at select people, but she'd never been shy. He didn't mind; it was just odd.

"She wants a cheeseburger meal," he told the cashier, an apology in his smile. "One that comes with a fairy toy."

The girl smiled back and nodded, her fingers flying over the screen of her register. "Good choice. Now . . ." She stepped to the side, away from the register, and leaned her elbows on the counter, her eyes on Hope. "I'm not telling everybody this, but we actually have two different fairies right now. I'm just supposed to put one in, but I think there's a particular one you would like. Am I right?"

Hope peeked out from Zane's side, her arms still clutching at him. She slowly nodded, her eyes wide.

"I thought so," their cashier drawled. "Tell me which one you want, and I'll make sure it gets in. But don't tell anybody else that I'm doing that, okay? It's our secret."

Zane glanced down to see Hope smiling just a little. "Do you have the green one?"

The girl winked, her smile spreading. "Sure I do. And because you're my new friend, you also get a free milkshake with your meal, if your daddy here says that's okay."

Hope tugged on Zane's jacket and looked up at him. "Can I get one, Daddy? Can I? A chocolate one?"

Zane looked at the cashier, brow raised. "You don't have to do that. I've worked behind the counter before, I know you can't just . . ."

"Oh, sure I can," she interrupted with a wave of her hand as she moved back to her screen. "Tuesday night promotions are fifty-cent milkshakes, and I have fifty cents right here. No biggie, and your little bug gets a bonus. Win-win. Y'all want another drink with that meal, or just the shake?"

Sensing this was not an argument worth having, Zane just smiled. "Fruit punch. Then I'll have a number five, large size, and a Coke."

"Dipping sauce?"

"For fries?" he asked with a disbelieving laugh.

The girl's eyes darted to his, a smile tucking against her cheeks. "Sir, you would not believe the random requests I get around here. Just ketchup, then?"

"Perfect." He pulled out a few bills from his wallet and handed them to her. "Keep the change. And thank you."

She winked again. "Sure thing. Now your number is thirty-seven, and if y'all will just slide your way down there, I'll have it up shortly. Bye now."

Sometimes Zane really loved the South. He put his arm around Hope and steered her towards the end of the counter. "That would almost never happen anywhere else, kiddo. I just want you to know that."

"She is my new favorite waitress *ever*," Hope gushed.

"Not sure she's actually called a waitress."

Hope didn't care; she just watched the goings-on behind the counter in anticipation of her food. She was practically bouncing in her sneakers as she tried to see everything, every detail of the preparation and the placement of the promised fairy toy.

Probably mostly for the fairy toy.

Zane watched her watching with some amusement. It wasn't often that he saw himself in his daughter, but this was exactly something he would have done. He had always loved seeing things from start to finish, whether it was a load of laundry, a race, or a batch of cookies in the oven. His mom had gotten after him more than once for sitting in front of the oven to watch her cookies bake, but it hadn't cured his curiosity even a little.

Or his drive.

It was one of the things that made him a great hockey player. At least, that was what he'd been told and what he believed. He played a game from beginning to end. No letting up, no brakes, no cutting corners. Start to finish, all in, all focus, all heart.

Apparently his baby girl had inherited that attribute as well. If she got anything from him, coloring aside, that was probably the best.

Just a few moments later, a tray with their order slid across to them, and Hope grabbed the tray with eager hands.

"Pump the brakes, baby cakes," he said quickly, taking the tray from her. "Let Daddy carry that, okay? You find us a table. Go ahead."

Still practically dancing, Hope skipped ahead of him, looking for an open table scattered among the mostly filled or half-filled tables. She finally found one right in the front and center of the rest, of course, and darted towards it with the same enthusiasm she had for everything else.

Maybe she'd also gotten that from him.

Hard to tell.

Zane followed her and set the tray down, pulling her food off and setting it before her. "Okay, Hopey-Dope, I've got a cheeseburger kids meal, toy inside, a fruit punch, and . . ." He paused and took a long sip of her milkshake.

"Hey!"

He exhaled in contentment and gave her a devious smile. "And one very good chocolate milkshake."

Hope heaved a dramatic sigh with an eye roll. "Daddy . . . that is mine."

"You are so right. I just needed to test it for you." He winked and put it down before her. "Get hoppin', girlfriend. I'll eat your fries if you don't finish them."

"Don't touch my fries," she ordered with a dark look.

He laughed and sat down, pulling out his own food. "Okay, I'll just eat mine, then."

"Yes. Do that." Hope suddenly turned her focus to her cheeseburger, and Zane did the same with his. It wasn't amazing, but it was certainly good enough. He'd feel fat and lazy afterwards, but he'd put in a run tonight after Hope was in bed to feel better.

Nothing crazy, just a few miles.

He could catch up on this week's TV shows he'd DVRed. That always seemed to make the time pass a bit easier.

"Daddy! Daddy, it's Miss Mara!"

Zane looked at his daughter, his mouth full with a too-big bite of burger. "What?" he managed to say around the bite.

His daughter pointed, her expression bright. "Look! Look, it *is* her!"

He looked where she was pointing, and sure enough, there was the tall, attractive woman from the gym, her dark bob sporting a braid across the top that draped behind one ear. Her face was almost completely devoid of makeup, which was refreshing and fitting, as the woman he had seen the other day hadn't needed any to enhance her looks. Oddly enough, now she wore a pair of navy-blue scrubs and tennis shoes.

So she wasn't a full-time fitness instructor. Intriguing.

"Miss Mara!" Hope called out, standing up and waving.

Zane looked at his daughter in shock. "Hope, honey, don't . . ."

It was too late; Mara had stopped and was scanning the

tables in confusion. Her eyes fell on Hope, and her expression changed instantly as she beamed.

The breath in Zane's lungs vanished at the sight.

*Wow.*

Mara came over to them, tray in hand, and tucked a strand of hair behind her ear. "Hiya, Hope! How are you?"

"Great! Daddy let me get a cheeseburger, and it came with a fairy toy!"

Mara gaped in an excellent display of disbelief. "No. Way. Why didn't anyone tell me? I would have gotten one!"

Hope giggled and shook her head. "They're for kids, silly. You can't have one."

"What?" Mara scoffed loudly, one hand going to her hip. "Well, that's not fair. It's not like I wanted to be a grown-up, it just happened. You sure I can't get one?"

"No." Hope laughed again.

"Shucks." Mara snapped her fingers, then looked over at Zane, her bright smile fading. "Hi, sorry, I should have . . ."

He rose way later than he should have, shaking his head. "No worries," he said in a rush, overriding whatever she had been about to say. "Zane. Winchester." He held out a hand.

She took it and shook quickly, her grip surprisingly firm, bumping her up at least ten points in his mind. "Mara Matthews. I teach Hope's Saturday kids' Zumba class."

"Right. Yeah, I remember." He smiled, more at the memory than at her.

Mara's cheeks colored quickly. "Right. Her coat the other day. Totally looking my best after four classes, all sweaty and frizzy and gross. Not exactly the greatest first impression."

"I didn't notice," he assured her, smiling further still. And truthfully, he hadn't. Of course he'd noticed she was in leggings and a baggy tank over a tighter one, and he'd certainly noticed the quality of the legs she walked on, and he'd noticed the perfection in her above-average height, and he'd noticed a strong jaw, incredible cheekbones, and the slightest dusting of freckles across the bridge of her nose and cheeks. But had he noticed anything resembling sweaty, frizzy, or gross?

Not at all.

He'd also noticed the affection she'd had for his daughter, which was more important than anything else he had seen.

Except for the legs, possibly.

They really were amazing.

Zane eyed her tray and could have laughed when he saw a burger and fries from the other burger place in the food court. "Good choice," he said with a head tilt towards her tray. "I'd have gone there myself if this one had let me."

"What?" Mara looked down at her tray, then snorted to herself. "Oh. Right, yeah, um . . . rough day at work called for comfort food. I'd have gotten a milkshake, too, only their machine was broken." She pouted and looked at Hope sadly. "I love milkshakes."

"Me too!" Hope grabbed hers and held it up. "They gave me one for free! You can have it."

Zane smiled as Mara's eyes widened. "What? No, sweetie, that's yours. You deserve it."

"We can share it!" Hope pointed at the third chair at their table. "Come sit down with us. We can all eat together and then we can share the milkshake!"

"I couldn't," Mara protested. "It's a daddy-daughter date, I'm not . . ."

"We can let someone else in our date," Zane interrupted again. He pressed his foot against the leg of the open chair and scooted it out. "Come on, join us."

She looked at him, a wrinkle in her brow, her lips thinning into a line.

"Please, Miss Mara?" Hope asked. "Please?"

Mara looked at Hope, her expression instantly softening. "That is completely unfair. You have the world's best puppy dog eyes. How does anybody ever say no to you?"

"They don't," Zane and Hope said together, she with brightness, he with resignation.

Exhaling a sound he couldn't interpret, Mara moved around the table, setting her tray down and sitting in the chair. "Right. Here's to a burger night at the mall."

"Here, Miss Mara." Hope slid her milkshake over to her. "You've *got* to try this."

"No, really, sweetie, it's fine." Mara smiled at her fondly. "I'll get a milkshake another time."

Hope frowned at her, her eyes narrowing. "Drink the milkshake."

Mara coughed in surprise and looked at Zane. "Where in the world does that stubborn streak come from? Right out of the blue."

"That would be me, I'm afraid," he admitted, making a face. "Although there are other genes we could blame for it too." He leaned closer to whisper, "You'd better do what she says. It's safer if you go along with it."

"Sounds like it." She reached for the milkshake and took a small sip, turning back to Hope. "Oh wow, that is *so* good!"

Hope grinned. "Told ya!"

"Hey, little miss," Zane said, tapping a finger on the table near her food. "Dinner. Much as we like Miss Mara, you need to eat."

She obediently picked up her burger and took a bite out of it, her attention drawn to the bag her meal came in and the puzzles on it.

Zane turned to Mara again. "Sorry about that. When she gets an idea, there's no stopping her."

Mara waved that off. "Don't worry about it. She's a sweet

girl, and I'll never complain about getting a milkshake out of the deal." She shrugged and took a bite out of her burger, moaning softly as she chewed. The moan cut off almost at once, and she covered her mouth with one hand. "I am so sorry. That's embarrassing."

"Not really," he replied with a chuckle, though he would admit to his spine tingling at the sound. "A good burger deserves to be appreciated. What do you have going on there?"

She turned it towards him so he could see. "Cheese, tomato, bacon, lettuce, mayonnaise, barbecue, crispy onions. They've got this amazing sauce over there that is so good. Like I-would-drink-it-from-the-bottle good." She screwed up her face and looked away. "Sorry, sorry. I'm an idiot, and I say things, and . . ."

"Please," he told her with a laugh. "I like people who are real. Real food, real reactions, real opinions. I'll flat out tell you my burger is just meh, but the fries are good. A little saltier than I like, but that's what I expect. And you enjoying that burger the way you are is making me really jealous."

"Sorry not sorry." Mara shrugged and looked at her burger with a smile. "I've earned this, even if the calories are crazy."

Zane laughed once. "Calories are a bad word. Just eat the food."

Mara gave him a look. "I teach fitness classes. Calories are the staple."

"You teach more than the kids' classes?" He raised a brow, sensing he might have her cornered here. "I don't think five-year-olds know what calories are."

Sure enough, Mara made a face. "No . . . no, and I'm not a fitness nut. I mean, working out is great and all, but I like carbs too much to worry about them. Not my fault, though. I was raised in a bakery."

Zane sat back in his chair, plucking a few fries and popping them in his mouth. "Really? Locally, or . . .?"

"Yep, born and bred in Nashville, couldn't you tell?" She gestured to her mouth, then tossed her hand in a helpless gesture.

The motion made him focus on her mouth, more particularly her lips, which were full enough to tempt him without being so full they were distracting. Perfect lips.

And the corner of one had a touch of barbecue sauce on it.

Just perfect.

He swallowed, cleared his throat, and grabbed more fries. "Do I know it?"

"Not sure. You know A Dash of Goodness?"

Zane sat forward at once. "You kidding? I love that place! I don't have much of a sweet tooth, but I am hooked on the scones."

Mara smiled knowingly. "You ever try the cinnamon rolls?"

"Uh, yeah. Killer." He exhaled in a rush, eyes widening for effect. "Seriously, though."

"So I hear." She smiled and picked up some fries of her own. "What brings you guys to the mall tonight?"

Zane sipped his drink and pointed towards Hope. "Little miss here has been begging to come out here for weeks now, and I had a free night between games. Her birthday is in a few weeks, and we have a tradition. We shop, and she points out what she wants. Makes it much easier for me."

"Genius," Mara told him with an approving nod. "You said between games. You coach?"

"Daddy plays hockey," Hope broke in, ketchup and mustard gathering at the corners of her mouth. "I watch him on TV sometimes."

Zane smiled at that, but slid his eyes to Mara warily. There was no knowing how anyone would react to that sort of revelation, especially when she clearly had no idea who he was.

Mara blinked, then looked at Zane, her expression not quite thunderstruck but almost. "Hockey? Professionally?"

He shrugged. "And now entering the ice, number twenty-one, right defender, Zane Winchester."

Mara shook her head slowly. "Well, that puts things into perspective."

"How so?"

"I tend to rank things," she admitted. "Levels, tiers, that sort of thing. Pro athlete puts you up here." She illustrated the point with her hand.

"Okay . . . so where are you on this scale?"

She lowered her hand dramatically. "Nurse. Right here."

Zane frowned at her, took her hand, and brought it up higher. "Here, at least. You have skills, experience, and education. I didn't go to college at all. Right out of high school, I went pro. I'm a grunt, and that's about it."

"Uh-huh, nice try." She turned her attention to her food and seemed to be in more of a hurry to eat. "I should go," she said after four bites. "I need to find a present for my mom and get home. It's been a long day, and . . ."

"Shop with us!" Hope suggested brightly. "Daddy needs to know what I want for my birthday, and we can help you find what your mom wants."

Mara tried for a smile, but it was clear she was uncomfortable with the idea. "No, I can't, sweetie. This is a time for you and your dad, and you'll need to get home too."

"Mara," Zane tried softly, not sure what had changed and why she was suddenly desperate to be away from them.

"I'm really good at picking out presents," Hope said. "And I never get to pick out presents for a mom. Just Dad. Please can I? Please?"

"Hope."

She looked at Zane, and he shook his head at her, though he felt his heart crack at the pain he heard in her voice, what he saw in her expression. It wasn't often she said anything about Michelle, but when she did . . .

"Okay, sweetie," Mara said softly, sitting back against her chair. "I'd love your help."

Zane exhaled slowly in relief and turned to thank Mara, only she wouldn't look at him. His brow furrowed at that.

What in the world was going on here?

# FOUR

"Don't watch it, don't watch it, don't watch it..."

The TV seemed to be staring back at her. Daring her. Tempting her.

Taunting her.

"No," she told the screen, drying off her hair with a towel. "Not happening. Not okay for me to want to watch, considering..."

She trailed off, her lips pursing.

Could she watch a hockey game just to check out the dad of one of her students? When he was clearly in a relationship?

She couldn't find much out on the internet, which was one of the greatest letdowns she'd known in recent years. What good was the wealth of information if she couldn't properly cyber-stalk an exceptionally attractive professional athlete?

There were plenty of pictures and details about Zane Winchester, that was true, and some very attractive photo shoot pics involving several good-looking athletes, but he seemed to be the best built out of the bunch.

Figures.

But she didn't want the pictures. Not initially, anyway, though she might have saved one or two into a folder on her computer. All she wanted to know was his relationship status. That was all.

Was that really too much to ask?

There was some speculation on the internet, but he was never pictured with anyone as a date. The only thing she could find was some old pictures from when he was first called up and from a few years ago with a short woman with fake-brown hair and a carefully constructed makeup routine of a face. She had been labeled as his wife then, but that wasn't the perfect woman from the gym.

Hope had said she never got to buy presents for a mom; was Perfection her dad's girlfriend? She seemed pretty close with Hope, but it was looking more and more like she hadn't given birth to Hope. So had the past wife been Hope's mom? Where was she? What had happened? Was she still Zane's wife?

This was where the internet had failed her.

Nothing about Zane's social life. Nothing. He wasn't a partier, and he wasn't such a huge name in hockey that female hockey fans started conversations or blogs speculating on his personal life. He wasn't on social media, and the only recent photos of him off of the ice she had found had been at some hockey club gala in Chicago.

He'd been gorgeous in a tux, and she hadn't known until her internet searching that he had a manbun. Normally that wasn't a look she went for, but on him . . .

It worked.

Absolutely worked.

The fade on the sides of his head helped to not make him look like a surfer or a bum and instead made him look like a model of a hockey player instead of an actual one.

Either way, she really wanted to see his hair unobstructed by a helmet or a baseball cap.

She'd never have the opportunity to do so, but she could wish.

Interestingly, there were no pictures of Hope on the internet. There wasn't a single mention of her at all. No indication that Zane was a dad. As far as the internet was concerned, Hope didn't even exist.

Zane Winchester might have been a showboat on the ice, according to reports and stories and such, but it seemed like he was a complete mystery off of it.

Why was that even more attractive?

Mara could have died five times over during that awkward evening at the mall. What was supposed to be a quick dinner and shopping trip after work had turned into a display of all of her quirks and insecurities in front of the single most attractive man she'd ever met. And his adorable, precocious daughter.

The moment he'd told her who he was, she'd felt like a moron. Not only was he a married man, or at least a taken one, but he was a professional athlete. Her comment about perspective hadn't been about occupation at all when it tumbled out of her mouth, but she had recovered well enough, she thought. That had been entirely about the dating league and where they stood in comparison. Had he been available at all.

And had been interested in Mara in the first place.

She didn't mind sitting at a table with Hope and Zane, not when Hope was such a fun part of her class, but there was something strange about getting to know the parent of a student when she didn't know the other parent. And when she found the parent she *did* know so intriguing.

Escaping from the situation had been the only thing she could think of, and rambling about buying a present for her mom was supposed to have been her ticket out of there. How could she have known Hope would latch onto the idea and want to come with? Or that Zane would agree?

Or that she'd wind up having a great time and eventually relax into easy conversation with him?

She'd forgotten that her hair was dirty and still in work mode and that she was walking around in the most unflattering scrubs she owned. She'd forgotten he was a pro athlete that shouldn't be able to remember her name. It hadn't felt like a date, or anything like that, especially with Hope there between them and asking all sorts of questions, but it had felt like they were friends who had happened to meet at the mall.

There had still been some awkward moments on Mara's part, of course, as she was incapable of functioning normally when she needed to, but those had been limited to saying more than she should and intentionally pretending she only needed to pay attention to Hope. It was so much easier to engage with her than with her dad, as was usually the case with kids. That was one of the reasons she taught classes for kids instead of adults; kids were so much easier to work with.

And talk to.

And wander a mall with.

But Zane had been okay, once she forgot he was Zane. If she didn't look at him, it was really easy to talk with him.

He was *insanely* tall, but she was six feet flat herself, so it wasn't often that guys were much taller than her.

She liked that Zane was that much taller than her.

She liked it a lot.

But no. No, no, no, she was not going to watch his game tonight despite the fact that she was now almost an expert in everything the internet had to say about him. She wasn't much of a hockey fan, so she didn't exactly understand a lot of what was said about him, but she got the gist of it.

Zane Winchester was an animal. The penalty king. The warmer of the penalty box. The world record holder in penalty attempts. The government's secret weapon of defense. The pro wrestler who got lost and found himself on the ice.

On and on it went, doing nothing for Mara's curiosity and confusing her more than anything else. The man she had met had been nothing but funny and kind. He doted on his daughter and went out of his way to make people comfortable. He was imposing to the $n$th degree, but once you talked with him, that decreased.

And he was supposed to be the scariest player on the ice? That didn't match up.

Maybe she should watch his game, if for no other reason than to understand how he could possibly have such a split personality. And to support the family of her student. It was a show of respect, wasn't it? Something she was really almost duty bound to do, if she cared about her classes at all.

Which, of course, she did.

So.

Biting her lip, Mara picked up the remote and switched on the TV, immediately finding the guide and scrolling for the right channel. Soon enough, the game was on her screen, and Mara was sitting cross-legged on her couch, leaning forward to watch.

Her first thought was that Zane wasn't on the ice.

Her second was that this game was *fast*.

Thankfully, her younger brother Conor had gone through a hockey phase when he was a kid, so she knew a little about the rules and positions. But that brief window of exposure was minimal at best, and the pace of the game couldn't even begin to be compared.

It took some getting used to, but eventually Mara could follow along, and right about the time that happened was when she noticed Zane on the ice.

When had that happened?

She shook her head at herself and focused. It didn't matter when he'd come into the game, he was there now. She could pay attention to one player, surely. That should be simple enough.

Just follow number twenty-one.

Five minutes of doing just that, and Mara suddenly knew what the internet had been talking about.

Zane Winchester was crazy.

He slammed players into the boards of the rink left and right, his hockey stick furiously moving along the ice between the skates of other players. He could be at mid-ice helping the offense and within a blink be back in their zone protecting their goal. He was fast on the ice, almost inhumanly so, but it was his aggression that took Mara by surprise.

The announcers kept referring to him as Zamboni, and she wasn't sure why, but it seemed to give him more of an edge than he already had. He knocked several players off their feet without any trouble and never seemed to lose footing himself. Every hit he made sent the crowd into a frenzy, and he seemed to relish in that. More than once she saw him trying to pump them up more, and that didn't seem to fit.

Those were the kind of athletes she'd never really cared for. Hot dogs, she'd always called them, and their antics were always accompanied by a massive roll of the eyes.

Yet there Zane was, tapping fists with his teammates on the bench as he skated by them to the penalty box.

She had no idea what the offense had been, but nobody seemed particularly surprised that he was headed there so early in the game.

"And really, Todd, you've gotta wonder why a team keeps a guy like Zamboni on their squad. Animal on the ice, but at what cost? A powerplay this early in the game against the

Bruins isn't exactly a good move," one of the commentators said.

"Well, I can see the beauty of having a bruiser on the team, John," came the reply. "The guy makes things happen, and there is no denying his skills with the stick either. He's strategic, even in his physicality, and most of the time, he knows right where the line is between playing hard and a penalty."

"Be that as it may, at some point, he's gotta be considered for a suspension. If he can't play clean, he shouldn't play."

Mara found herself glaring at the screen, though the commentators weren't visible now that play had resumed on the ice.

"He *can* play clean, John. The question everybody has really got to ask is what does Coach Winkler see in Zamboni? He knows exactly what he is dealing with there, and he's hanging onto him. That's gotta speak for itself."

Mara nodded in agreement, then caught herself and scowled at nothing in particular. She didn't know Zane or his playing well enough to be agreeing on this particular subject, or any other subject, but this seemed fair enough. What she knew of the Tennessee Hounds program was that their coach was an up-and-comer, a cowboy in the coaching world, and he seemed to be making some strides with the team. When Mara was growing up, their team had been a bit of a joke, but no one laughed about them now. They might not have made it to the championships yet, but they had certainly proven themselves a formidable opponent.

The last few years especially.

Could that have something to do with Zane? She wasn't naive enough to think he could carry an entire team into victory, especially when he was a defender and not likely to score a goal at any given time. But there was something to be said for a player's attitude and drive and for the ability of those qualities to motivate an entire team.

Mara watched Zane as best as she could while he sat in the penalty box, though it wasn't like the cameraperson had any interest in a player not currently on the ice. From what she could tell, he watched every move on the ice and cheered his teammates on. He didn't seem overly concerned about being in there, and somehow, he wasn't distracted by the fans clamoring for him around the penalty box.

Completely focused on the game, even when he wasn't in it.

Interesting.

Okay, so he pounded on the plexiglass behind him once or twice, and when his teammates did something that got the crowd going, he gestured for them to get louder. But his eyes were always on the ice.

And somehow, his team scored a goal during the penalty, despite being down a man.

The crowd went ballistic.

The announcers were lost.

"I don't even know how that's possible, John. How do you score a goal on a team like this when you are down a man, especially when that man is Zamboni?"

"Todd, I'm sure the Bruins are asking themselves that same question. You might want to ask Coach Wink what other tricks he has up his sleeve, because there is no way Zamboni's penalty was an accident after a move like that. We've gotta watch this team and this coach, folks, because there is magic in the air in Tennessee!"

Mara found herself grinning at the screen, disappointed that she wasn't at the arena with the fans watching this game in person. What an insane moment.

"And with the goal, the teams line up again, still without

Zamboni. Forty-five more seconds for him. Since the team with the advantage was not the team who scored, the two-minute penalty does not end. Not unheard of in hockey but certainly not that common, and certainly not against a tough team like the Bruins."

"You're absolutely right, John, and the Bruins have gotta be smarting after that, so the Hounds need every advantage they have. Zamboni's chomping at the bit in there, you can just see how much he wants to be back out there now that the play is done."

"If his team can hold off an angry Bruins squad with an advantage, we're going to get one amped-up Zamboni out there to make up for lost time."

There was a laugh from the commentators. "An amped-up Zamboni. Considering the level he already plays at, what would amped up look like for him?"

"Todd, I don't wanna know."

They laughed again, and Mara laughed with them.

Why, she didn't know, but she knew she'd be pulling out her phone to track down some Hounds clothing to wear when the game went to intermission. She might have been ambivalent about the team before, but she was completely invested now.

There wasn't anything wrong with that, right?

She was a Tennessee girl. She could cheer for a Tennessee team without it meaning anything in particular.

She should have been watching them a long time ago, if she was honest. But better late than never, and she'd be able to thank Hope Winchester for that.

Not her dad.

He hadn't been the one to tell her he played for them; he'd only confirmed it. Hope had told Mara he played hockey.

What would Zane have said?

Finally, his penalty was up and he skated out of the box with an almost frenzied edge to his motion. Mara bit back a squeal, her hands going to her lap in excitement as she watched him race towards his team's zone. He swept to the right and clocked an opponent hard into the boards, then darted behind the goal, scooping up the puck and sending it screaming around the boards, out of danger and into the hands of a teammate who could continue the momentum forward.

Mara released a breath she hadn't known she'd been holding and sank back against the couch roughly.

How pathetic was she? Hanging on by a thread over a team she couldn't have cared about before this, just because she had met one guy on the team.

One guy. One very tall, very hot, very adorable dad of a hockey player whose relationship status was unidentifiable and whose daughter Mara would see in class on Saturday.

One guy, and now she was hooked on this sport and this team.

Absolutely pathetic.

She moodily watched as Zane and his co-defender skated to the bench while two others came on, managing only a weak smile as she watched him bump fists with a few of the teammates there.

Falling for a guy at first look was one thing; falling for a guy she could never, would never, should never have—for more reasons than she had fingers—was just wrong.

She was supposed to be beyond this stupidity now.

Hadn't she been through enough faux relationships in her life to learn that lesson?

A tinny version of elevator music sounded, and Mara glanced around for her cell phone. After fumbling between the cushions, she pulled it out, glanced at the screen, and hit the answer button.

"Hi, Mama," she said in a falsely bright tone, grabbing the remote and muting the game.

"Hey, Mars. What are you doing tonight? I'm not interrupting, am I?"

Mara rolled her eyes and stared up at the ceiling. "I wouldn't have answered if you were interrupting."

"Well, I don't know, maybe you need an escape phone call," her mom suggested, a teasing note in her voice. "That does happen, you know."

"On dates, Mama. People need escape calls on dates."

"I know that."

Mara heaved a sigh. "You have to go on dates to need an escape call on a date."

"So go on a date."

"Did you just call me to see if I was dating?" Mara demanded as she ran her fingers along her scalp in a sort of massage.

Her mother laughed once. "Of course not! What are you doing now?"

Mara bit her lip, chewing in hesitation for a moment. "Watching a Hounds hockey game."

"Really?" her mother asked in surprise. "Why?"

"One of the little girls in my class has a dad on the team," she replied truthfully. "Thought I'd check it out."

More like check *him* out, but her mother didn't need to know that.

"Oh! Your father has been watching the Hounds this season. Who's the player?"

Mara hissed and winced. "Not sure I should tell you, Mama. They're really private about the whole thing. Like really private."

"You can tell me, Mars. I won't tell your father, and nobody I know likes hockey."

That was true, and her mother was a vault when it came to secrets, unlike any of her siblings. But still . . .

"It's not my secret to tell, Mom," Mara said softly. "I don't know them well, so you really need to keep this quiet."

"I can do that, hon. Croissant my heart."

Mara smiled, laughing softly at the old family joke. Bakery life was just special, and no one outside of it would really get it. "That serious?"

"Sounds like it should be."

"It should." Mara took in a quick breath. "It's Zane Winchester. His daughter, Hope, is in my class."

Her mother made a noncommittal sound. "I'll keep my eyes open when I catch snippets of the game with your dad. The name means nothing to me, but I'm sure I'll find him."

"He's kind of hard to miss, Mom," Mara replied with a laugh. "He's the one who's always knocking people over and slamming them into the boards."

"Oh my. An aggressive guy. Be careful."

Mara shook her head, though her mom wouldn't be able to see that. "He's not like that in person. You should see him with his little girl. So sweet and funny, and she just adores him."

"Sounds like you like him yourself."

Yikes. That obvious?

"I like any guy who treats his daughter like that," Mara told her with real honesty. "I ran into them at the mall the other night, and he didn't pull out his cell phone once. Hope had his entire attention."

"Now that sounds like a guy I would like. Consider me a fan."

"I'm sure he'll be pleased to hear it. If I ever see him again, I'll be sure to tell him." She looked at the TV again, wondering how long Zane would be off the ice. The front line had switched twice now without him coming back out, and the game wasn't as fun without him out there. The team was just as good but not particularly exciting.

Interesting.

"Would you go to a hockey game with me, Mama? Soon?" Mara heard herself ask. "Daddy can come too, and we can invite others, but it might be fun with just us."

"I think that would be a fun night! Let me talk with your father, but I don't see why he wouldn't want to. We'll have to get ourselves some team shirts, though. I've seen the stands when he watches the home games, and there is no way we can enter that place without team apparel. How about their next home game?"

Mara grinned as Zane and his co-defender came back out onto the ice, drawing her knees up to her chest as her heart pattered a little. "I think I can handle that. What kind of team apparel did you have in mind?"

# FIVE

"Oh yay. Overtime. My favorite."

"Shut up."

"That's not a nice word."

"That's because it's two words, genius."

"Cut it out, both of you."

"Yes, Mother."

Zane grinned at Boomer, his co-defender, and he grinned back. They were in a ridiculous mood tonight, and when they got into bantering, Shap got bossy. He was the captain, so he had a right to it, but Zane and Boomer never let him get too far.

Shap was tense with the tie at the end of the third, going into overtime, and Zane could understand that. There was no way they should have tied, not with the power they had in their front lines. But the Eagles had a goalie that was on fire tonight, and though they had outshot the Eagles at least three to one during the game, the score was only two apiece.

Not a great night for them.

Zane, for one, was exhausted. They'd been on the road for days and got stuck in Denver while a snowstorm cleared out on their way back from LA. They'd gotten home in time to keep their game with the Eagles on the docket, but without much actual rest for the team. He wouldn't blame their performance tonight on that, but it certainly wasn't helping.

He'd hide that as much as he could. He was a veteran player, known for high energy no matter what, and times like these were when it mattered most.

But when three guys on the bench were hiding yawns, motivation would need to be something epic if it were to have any effect.

The buzzer sounded the end of the third period, and Zane was the first one on his feet, thumping his stick against the ground to the tempo of the crowd's chants. His teammates picked up on it and kept it going, the crowd behind the box catching the beat.

Zane grinned as his teammates on the ice skated towards them, coming off for intermission but hearing the stomping the crowd was sending up.

"Come on!" Zane bellowed, turning to the crowd and gesturing with his arms.

As he'd hoped, a sort of wave started as people got to their feet, carrying the rhythm to another level as they stomped and clapped, the sound wrapping around the arena, rippling among the crowd. The once relatively sleepy spectators were now almost all on their feet, team banners waving above heads.

"Nice," Boomer commented as they followed their teammates out of the box and into the locker rooms. "Think they can ride that until we come back out?"

"They better," Zane muttered to him. "Between staying awake and staying in the game, I'm not sure I've got it in me."

Boomer grunted and tapped his helmet in solidarity. They headed into the locker room with the rest, and Zane was happy to see that there was a little more pep in the step of his teammates and that no one looked as tired as he felt.

If they could just skate it out in overtime long enough to score, they could all get the rest they wanted so much.

Zane removed his helmet and shook his head hard, exhaling roughly as he sat down at his locker.

He was going to miss bedtime tonight. That happened every now and then, but he didn't like it. Hope's life had been disrupted enough as it was.

Leaning back into his locker a touch, he reached for his phone to text Josie and, by extension, Hope. A missed call caught his eye, and he swiped for more info.

*Michelle.*

He stared at the screen longer than he should, his frown deepening, his emotions exploding in seven different directions.

What the hell did she want?

She hadn't left him a message, so it couldn't be that important. If she was going to argue the alimony amounts one more time, she could talk to his lawyer, just as she had all the other times. His case was ironclad, and unless she decided to take her parenting of Hope seriously, nothing was going to change.

"Heads up," Flake, his locker neighbor, muttered with a nudge.

Zane glanced up to see Coach Wink head in, and he zipped off his auto message for situations like these. Josie would get it, and he'd make up for it with Hope tomorrow night.

Hopefully, his punishment would be only two more books than normal. Last time, she'd made him sing her songs, and he'd had to make some up, which had done nothing to put her to sleep but everything to keep her giggling way past her bedtime.

He knew it would come back to haunt him one day; it was only a matter of time.

Sliding the phone into his bag, he tuned back in to the present and listened attentively as Coach Wink gave them their strategy and marching orders.

He would admit to being slightly distracted, though.

He ground his teeth at the thought of Michelle, that same old flare of anger and resentment hitting his gut. He shook his head to himself, forcing a slow exhale through his nose. He didn't need any more complications in his life than he'd already had, and he certainly didn't need them just as he'd finally seemed to find a groove.

"Dude, I can practically see the smoke coming out of your ears," Flake mumbled beside him.

Zane only nodded once, keeping his jaw tense. *Good.* More hockey to play meant more opportunities to drive his fury out of him on the ice. There was nothing like slamming his opponent or saving the day to revitalize himself at a time like this.

Might as well put his life's drama to good use.

Coach Wink clapped his hands twice, then gestured for them all to head back out to the ice. The team rose, pumping each other up and doing everything they could to get their energy higher. They could finish this game quickly if they focused, and Zane, for one, was all focus.

He said nothing as they moved back out into the arena, and his team seemed to sense the energy, the raw anger, thrumming through his frame.

Shap put a hand to his chest before they reached the ice.

Zane met his eyes.

"No penalties," Shap told him firmly. "We can't afford a man down like this."

Zane tilted his chin down, meeting the shorter player's

eyes almost squarely. "Then don't leave me time to get any. End it."

For a second, he thought the serious captain would crack a smile for that, but Shap only nodded in understanding, and the two of them skated out with the rest. Shap might not like Zane all the time, might find his antics annoying, and Zane might find him to be a little pretentious. But there was a mutual respect for each other's skills, and each well knew what the other was capable of. And what they could do together.

Sometimes hockey was a beautiful thing.

Zane skated around in easy waves over to his position, nodding at Boomer and Pike, who was settled in his goal like a caged animal. None of them wanted to be in this overtime for long, and it would take a concentrated effort from them all to make it happen.

Giving one sharp whistle, Zane lowered himself into a ready stance. "Here we go, Clay! Light 'em up, kid!"

Clay squared off against the Eagles' center, and Shap to his left seemed to be muttering encouragement under his breath. Zane flicked his eyes to Janny on the right and smirked when he saw the exact same intensity on his face as he saw on every other player on the ice.

This was going to be fun.

The puck was dropped, and Clay swept the puck away from center ice, sending it back to Zane, who scooped it up almost lazily. He moved forward on the ice, his eyes scanning for any and all players. The Eagles' left winger was coming at him hard, and it was exactly what Zane wanted.

"Hot, hot," Zane called, flinging the puck up into clear ice just as his attacker was reaching him, knowing Janny would be there in a heartbeat to grab it.

Zane stooped low and slammed his shoulder into the stomach of the Eagles' winger, sending him flying backwards and landing flat on his back on the ice, his stick sliding across the ice to the boards.

The crowd roared its approval, and Zane pumped a fist in the air as he took off towards center ice, Boomer sweeping behind him to cover.

"Yeehaw!" Boomer whooped as he moved by him. "That'll smart later!"

Zane grinned but focused his attention on the wingers and on Clay up near the goal.

They weren't making much happen, despite several shots on goal. It wasn't for want of trying; the Eagles were apparently just as hungry for this overtime as they were.

Something special would need to happen, if anything.

An Eagles player sent the puck around the boards, and Zane exhaled shortly, seeing an opening for something they'd only ever practiced once.

If there was ever a time to nail it, this was it.

"E-I-E-I," he shouted hoarsely as he raced towards the puck. "E-I-E-I!"

There was a pause for maybe the space of half a heartbeat, and then everyone moved. Boomer darted towards middle ice while the wingers charged forward and began scuffling against Eagle players in the offensive zone. Clay, on the other hand, swept up to meet Zane as he moved towards goal, the pair of them sending the puck between each other as they skated in parallel formation.

"Door! Door!" Boomer came forward and took on the large Eagles' center, currently keeping Janny busy while the Eagle defenders were focusing on intercepting Clay and Zane.

Janny dropped towards goal. "Over, over, over!"

As they'd hoped, one of the Eagle wingers moved to flank Janny, leaving Shap free to join Clay and Zane.

"Set?" Zane grunted.

"Go!" Clay and Shap said together.

Zane made a hard cut to the right, slapping the puck forward so that it wrapped around the boards behind the goal. He slammed the nearest Eagles' player into the boards, then spun around, hovering and starting to move backwards towards the net if they needed him to.

Boomer had done his job, and Janny had scooped the puck up from his side of the boards, sending it up to Boomer, who returned it to the right side, where Clay and Shap were.

Clay took possession and flicked the puck just inside the goalpost before the goalie could get there.

The buzzer sounded, and the entire arena roared its approval.

Zane whooped and rushed forward, almost skipping on the ice towards his teammates. They came together and pounded each other's backs and helmets.

"Good catch, Z!" Shap shouted, thumping his helmet hard. "Fantastic!"

"Hey, no penalties, eh?" Zane replied with a slap to his chest.

They turned towards the box, where their team was pounding the boards in celebration, making the accompanying barnyard sounds the play called for.

Zane threw his hands up into the air, whooping loudly. His teammates reciprocated, and he turned to skate along the boards towards their goal, whooping again and gesturing for the crowd to do the same.

The response was electric, and the trademark howl of a hound dog echoed across the speakers, followed by the equally important song that always accompanied a Hounds' win.

Pulling off his helmet, Zane exhaled deeply, tossing his head and pumping one fist in the air as he made his way behind the goal. Fans pounded the plexiglass as he did so, and he grinned at them all. Once he passed the goal, he skated backwards towards center ice, showing off a little, but the crowd loved it. He pointed at a particularly loud section with his stick, raising his helmet in his other hand as if to punch the rafters with it. They roared and clanged their cowbells, gold- and black-streaked faces practically glowing with excitement.

Zane laughed and lowered his arms, his eyes sliding just to the right of the section he'd riled, and saw a trio of people tucked in a section almost alone, as others around them had left. They were all on their feet and clapping, wearing the faux-jersey sweatshirts of black and gold, but that wasn't what caught his attention.

It was the tall brunette in the middle of the trio, her bobbed hair braided back with gold ribbons and her long, perfect legs encased in faded skinny jeans.

*Mara.*

He pointed directly at them, laughing, surprised at the exhilaration that hit him in the chest.

Mara's companions, an older man and woman, raised their hands above their heads as they clapped, but Mara kept her hands where they were. Her smile, however, could have lit the entire arena.

He needed to see her. Really see her.

He glanced behind himself to see the teams lining up and knew he needed to get back, but he couldn't—wouldn't—let this go. He looked back up at Mara, holding one hand up as the other pointed towards her.

Her head cocked to one side.

Perfect.

He pointed towards his right twice, then signaled the number twenty-two before pointing again.

She held up her hands in a helpless gesture.

Zane groaned as he skated backwards. He pressed his hands in a praying motion.

The man to Mara's left turned to say something to her, and then she nodded. Looking at Zane again, she nodded more emphatically.

He dipped his praying hands in gratitude, then spun to bring up the rear of his team's lineup to shake hands.

Slapping the palms of each guy he passed, Zane caught sight of the rookie he'd sent to his back and grinned at him. "All right there, Five?"

The kid gave him a crooked smile. "Breathing hurts, but I took on a Zamboni, right?"

Zane chuckled and cuffed the guy's head. "Dead on, buddy. Good luck, and stay hungry, 'kay?"

"Thanks, Z."

Zane nodded and moved on, slapping hands and giving a respectful nod to their captain, Danny Ream, who had been one of his fiercest competitors back in the Northbrook days.

"Once a cat, now a dog?" came the teasing remark. "Interesting."

"Well, we can't all go from firebirds to eagles, can we?" Zane replied, taking the time to actually shake his hand. "You guys are beasts. Do me a favor and pound the Steers for me, yeah?"

Danny laughed once. "Paper beats rock every time, bro. I got a score to settle."

Zane chuckled as well. "Tell him hi."

"Z-style?"

"Is there any other way?" Zane shook his hand again, then shook hands with the coaches, who didn't care all that much, before making his way towards the locker room. His eyes returned to where he had seen Mara, only to find the section empty.

He could only hope she'd gotten the message.

And would comply.

After taking the fastest shower known to professional athletes anywhere, Zane only paused long enough for an extra two swipes of deodorant before shouldering his bag and grabbing his coat. His teammates were used to him leaving before the majority of them, so they only waved at him as he left the locker room.

He hadn't been able to take a real breath since the game ended, and he hadn't exactly breathed much in overtime, so his heart pounded just as hard now as it had during those last few seconds. His chest ached still, and he knew that wouldn't really relax until he was in his bed tonight, but hopefully he would avoid panting in front of Mara and her parents.

It could be taken in so many wrong ways.

Not that panting over Mara would be wrong.

He frowned at that. He barely knew Mara; how would he know panting over her wouldn't be wrong?

*Legs,* his memory reminded him.

He slapped himself on the back of the head. He'd been a shallow guy once before, and only one good thing had come from that. He couldn't afford to be shallow, shortsighted, or immature anymore.

Much as he enjoyed a good pair of legs.

He glanced down at himself quickly, forgetting for a moment what he was wearing. Home games he didn't have to dress up as much, so he usually didn't, but thankfully, good jeans and a gray T-shirt were classic enough. His hair was still wet, but he'd put it up in a tidy bun, so he shouldn't look too scraggly.

Pausing for a moment, he dropped his bag and slipped his arms into his black leather jacket, despite still sweating and not really wanting to. Appearances with fans were important.

And, of course, there was Mara.

Over whom he would not pant.

He picked up his bag and hurried over to the end of the hall, then down just a few halls to gate twenty-two, which was the nearest any fan could get without being invited to the players' entrance.

He'd get her a pass.

His next step was slow as that thought bounced around in his mind. He'd get her a . . . Why in the world would he get her a pass?

Or anything?

Zane glanced up and couldn't help the grin that flashed across his lips. Leaning against the cement wall, one long leg propped up and bouncing slightly, was Mara. The other two adults stood nearby, purses on the ground next to a huge pillar, and all were chatting quietly, though Mara looked slightly uncomfortable.

He wasn't exactly at ease himself, but he had to do this. Not sure why, but he knew he did.

"You got the message," he said without any preamble whatsoever, surprising himself with his stupidity, his attention focused on Mara.

Her eyes darted to his at once. "You did say please. Sort of."

He smiled easily, his discomfort fading a little. "I tried. The crowd made asking out loud a little difficult."

"Wonder whose fault that was." She smiled just a little at him, and that little smile made his stomach backflip precisely three times.

He covered it by turning to the couple at the pillar. "I'm so sorry, where are my manners? Zane Winchester." He extended his hand, walking towards them.

"Paul Matthews," the man said, grinning as he took Zane's hand. "Mara's father. This is my wife, Vicki."

Zane offered his hand to her as well, mentally smirking

at how alike Mara and the woman looked, despite her being twenty-plus years older. Like seeing into the future. "A pleasure, ma'am."

"Bless you, sweetie, the pleasure's mine," Mrs. Matthews drawled in the most Tennessee twang he had ever heard.

For some reason, that made him smile more.

"Helluva finish to that game, son," Mr. Matthews said with an approving nod as Zane took a polite step back.

"Daddy," Mara interrupted with some exasperation. "Don't call him son!"

Mr. Matthews looked at her, one graying brow raising. "Mara June, I'll call 'em like I see 'em, and I'll thank you to shut your piehole."

She gaped at him, then covered her face as she burst out laughing. "Oh my gosh."

Mr. Matthews grinned up at Zane and winked. "Embarrassing daughters is one of the perks of being a father, Mr. Winchester."

Zane barked a laugh and nodded. "Please, sir, call me Zane. And I am well aware. Your daughter has the impossible job of teaching my little girl Zumba, and I don't envy her that. No one dances in our family."

Mrs. Matthews sobered and slipped her arm through her husband's. "I understand you are a private man, Zane, especially with your baby girl. Lord bless you for that. I had to drag that information out of Mara. I just want to assure you that we will not say a word about her, and you can trust us to take that to the grave."

There was something incredibly touching about that, and Zane looked over at Mara, whose hands had come down from her eyes and now rested at her mouth, her index fingers pulling the lower lip out slightly.

Amazing how distracting that was.

"I believe you," Zane murmured, his attention still on Mara.

As though she could hear him looking, her eyes came back to him. She straightened fully and dropped her hands, though her lower lip still fascinated him. "I wasn't sure . . ." she began before stopping and biting that lip with perfect teeth. "I didn't know what to tell them about why we . . . how we . . . and I didn't want to presume . . ."

"It's fine," Zane assured her gently. He smiled with genuine warmth and looked at her parents again. "I'm not worried about Hope where you three are concerned. The rest of the world, maybe. But not you." His eyes drifted back to Mara as she came closer to her parents.

And to him.

"Not you," he murmured again, this time for her alone.

The corner of her lips curved in another slight smile, and again, his stomach flipped.

Then it growled.

"I'm famished," he announced to no one in particular, looking around at them. "Can I take you guys out to dinner? Drinks? I've already missed bedtime, thanks to overtime, and it would be great to have some company not asking me to braid their hair or read *Princess Dolly and the Angry Apples* again."

"Depends on your braiding skills," Mara quipped in a low voice, as though she'd intended to keep the remark to herself.

Zane looked at her, lifting a brow in a challenge. "French, fishtail, upside-down, Dutch, or regular, smartie?"

Mr. Matthews chortled into a fist while Mrs. Matthews looked between Zane and Mara with a smile.

Chastened, but not beaten, Mara pursed her lips, and Zane wondered faintly if her perfect teeth were biting her cheek. She cleared her throat. "But can you do the *Princess Dolly* voices? Not worth reading if you don't."

"I'm going to ask your parents to drop you off at home if you keep this up," Zane told her, though there wasn't enough money in his contract to tempt him to follow through on that threat. He was enjoying this far too much, and he wanted it to continue for the rest of the night, if not longer.

"Excellent," Mr. Matthews replied, rubbing his hands together. "More *Angry Apple* voices for me."

Zane threw up his hands with a laugh, and the rest joined in. Mara, for one, was rosy cheeked, and there was something incredibly attractive about that.

*Please say yes.*

"Sorry," Mara told him with a hint of a wince. "It's late, and I've got an early shift tomorrow. We really should go."

A boulder landed in Zane's gut at that. "Really?"

Her blue eyes widened at the dejected tone, and he saw her swallow. "Sorry."

"But thank you so much for offering," Mrs. Matthews added smoothly, drawing Zane's attention. "Such a kind thought. But you go on home and get some rest. You've earned it."

Zane returned her smile, despite his disappointment. "Thank you, ma'am. Do you think you'll come to more games this season?"

"Oh, you can count on it," Mr. Matthews assured him. "Especially now that we've met you."

"Excellent." Zane grinned now, the weight lifting from him. "Well, I'll make sure Will Call has tickets in your name every home game."

"You don't have to do that," Mara said quickly while her parents only gaped.

"Sure I do," Zane corrected her. "I don't have much

family, or any particular fans, in Tennessee. Might as well give the seats to someone worthy of sitting in them." Again, he looked at Mara, daring her to take his meaning.

She said nothing, eyes still wide.

"Well, we won't keep you," Mrs. Matthews said, saving them all from the heavy silence. "Wonderful game, Zane. I hope we see you again soon."

"I hope so too, Mrs. Matthews," he told her with a dip to his chin. "I really do."

"Bye, then." Mara gave him a quick wave and turned, walking away, her parents following at a more sedate pace.

Zane watched her go, his eyes narrowing.

There was something very appealing about Mara Matthews, and he was suddenly desperate to figure out just what it was.

And to then explore that appeal in great depth.

# SIX

"Wrap it up, two, three, four, and take it back, two, three, four. Clap, touch, clap, touch, clap-clap-clap-clap-clap-clap-clap-clap, and punch!"

The kids cheered loudly, their fists high in the air, and Mara laughed, applauding their most exuberant dance in some time. They had come to class with their own selections of music, and she had done what she could with most, if not all of them. The class might not be its most effective exercise, but it was certainly the most entertaining.

Sometimes that was more important.

"Great job, you guys!" Mara told them, moving over to the stereo to change the song. "After all of that, I think we need a cooldown."

"What's a cooldown?" one of the kids asked loudly.

Mara grinned in her direction. "You know how you feel all hot and sweaty right now? A cooldown helps take that away, and it's good for your body in the process. Makes the body happy. Sound good?"

"Yeah!" a few kids cheered, while others looked uncertain.

"Hmm." Mara pursed her lips and looked around, seeing that she would have to do some convincing. How did one convince high-strung kids to do a cooldown? If any of them had athletic ideals for their lives, they'd need to swear by the cooldown or endure the consequences.

A slow smile crossed her lips at a memory from the night before, almost unrelated yet perfectly inspirational.

Mara pressed the play button and moved back to the front of the room. "Okay, cooldown music is starting, and Hope, can you come help me?"

Hope grinned and left her faux twin Claire to come up beside Mara, her braided pigtails bouncing wildly.

Gosh, this girl was adorable. Mara grinned down at her, amazed at how much of Zane she could see there.

*Gah. No Zane. Not here, not now.*

"Okay," she said quickly as she faced the class again. "First up: stretch up really high on your toes and try to reach your head to the sky."

The result would have been hilarious if anyone were recording it.

"Tiptoes, tiptoes, stretch the neck . . ." Mara told them, barely restraining laughter. "And now your arms are elephant trunks, hang 'em down!"

The kids all drooped their arms, swinging them from side to side, almost dragging their hands across the floor. They giggled as their arms bumped into each other, and a few started making elephant noises.

Mara smiled as she watched them, loving the entertainment they found in the simplest things. "And now we are gorillas! Swing those arms forward and walk!"

A bunch of imitation gorillas strode around the room, grunting and making all kinds of faces. A few of the boys thumped their chests, making Mara chuckle.

"Sloths!" Mara called out, dropping down to all fours. "Verrrrrrry slowwwwwww in everyyyyyyythinggggggg."

Now the giggles were everywhere as motions became exaggerated and slow, arms and legs stretching out dramatically. A few kids even turned on their backs and pretended the sloth was running upside down. Slowly, of course.

Random, but it worked.

Mara whistled loudly, bringing them all back to her. "Now be a seal!" She lay on her stomach, then arched her back, pointing her nose to the ceiling. "A circus seal. You have to balance an ice cream cone on your nose!"

"Seals don't balance ice cream cones!" Hope giggled beside her, trying to mimic the movement.

"This one does," Mara shot back. "Who else is doing it? Arf!"

Barks around the room echoed back to her, followed by more giggles.

"Swimming frog!" Mara balanced on her stomach and did a slow frog kick and stroke in the air.

This one was harder for the kids, but they went for it, as usual, and ribbits and croaks, of course, came with it.

Shaking her head, Mara exhaled, glancing up at the clock. "Okay, and who can tell me what an ostrich does with sand?"

"Puts its head down in it!" Claire called out.

"That's right, so now . . ." She pushed her hips up in the air, keeping her head and hands down by the floor. "We're ostriches with our heads in the sand!"

This one the kids loved, and they laughed at seeing each other upside down.

Mara looked over at Hope, who looked over at her. "Hey, upside-down Hope. How are you?"

Hope snickered and knocked one of her dangling braided pigtails out of her face. "Hi, upside-down Miss Mara. I'm fine!"

"Oh. I thought you were Hope, but hi, Fine!" Mara winked as Hope laughed again.

Lowering her hips, Mara rolled herself to a seated position and clapped her hands, grinning widely. "Okay, kiddos, we are done! Don't forget your jackets and water bottles. You can head on out of here, and make sure you visit Miss Hannah for your treat!"

The kids cheered and called out their thanks as they started to move from the floor to their belongings along the wall.

Mara sighed to herself and craned her neck, one hand gripping the back of it tightly.

Sleep last night had not been kind to her, and there was one reason for that. Just one.

Zane Winchester.

More specifically, guilt over Zane Winchester.

As fun as the game last night had been, as amazing as it was to watch him play, as exhilarating as it was to be with him afterwards . . . there was guilt. There was so much guilt she hadn't eaten breakfast.

She was fluttery, flustered, and flirting with Zane Winchester.

*Flirting.*

Mara didn't even know how to flirt! She was just awkward and bantering, snarky as her usual defense mechanism against embarrassment, and it wasn't until she was grinning, squealing, and flushed on the drive home that she had recognized the thing for what it was.

The Mara Matthews rendition of flirting.

*Horrifying* didn't even begin to describe what had washed over her then. A man who was by all accounts spoken for, whose daughter was her student, who happened to hit it off with her parents better than any of Mara's boyfriends ever had, who played professional hockey like he was the god of ice combined with the Gorgon who fought the god of ice, and who looked like the epitome of temptation and gloriousness before, during, and after said fight.

Her cheeks flamed, and she fanned herself, swallowing hard and wishing her bottle of water were beside her instead of across the room. Not to drink but to dump over her head.

"Did the cooldown not work for you, Miss Mara? You're still all red."

Mara looked up at the concerned face of Hope Winchester and felt her ears heat more than her face had. "I'm always red for longer than I should be, sweetie. I'm fine."

"Okay," Hope said slowly, and too knowingly for a girl of five. "Can I stack the mats for you?"

That softened Mara, and she smiled. "That would be wonderful. Thank you."

She watched as Hope picked up the puzzle-piece-shaped mats and began stacking them in the corner.

Such a sweet girl from such a sweet man.

Sweet in behavior, sweet for the eyes . . .

That chilling, sick feeling dropped back down Mara's throat and into her stomach, making her sway where she sat.

She was doomed, and she would be doomed until she could make this right. She had been up half the night trying to find a way to atone for her error of judgment and behavior, her sin against humankind, and the stain upon her character.

Confession.

Except confession came with confrontation, which was not Mara's favorite thing in the world. In fact, it was her least favorite thing in the world. It was actually the thing that she had spent her entire life avoiding, both in childhood and adulthood. She was very, very good at avoiding confrontation.

And now she was taking it on. Directly. Intentionally. Willingly.

To confess. About her fascination with Zane Winchester. And at least seven dreams about him.

Maybe eight.

She closed her eyes, exhaling slowly, hoping a quick meditation might help her to get over this sensation that she was going to throw up and die a painful death.

If a quick meditation was a thing.

*Inhale... Exhale... Inhale... Exhale...*

"Hopey-Dope, time to skedaddle, babes. Full day ahead."

Mara's throat clenched in a terrifying spasm as her eyes flew open, moving to the doorway to the room at once.

Perfection stood there, perfectly coordinated, perfectly glistening, perfectly smiling.

There was a zit forming on Mara's chin just from her envy, she was positive.

And possibly her guilt.

It was time.

Mara got to her feet, her kneecaps suddenly gone and her toes numb. But she walked on those wobbly, gangly, kneecap-less legs and moved to face Perfection head on, even while her ears felt like they were actually pulling her backwards. Away from confrontation, confession, and perfection.

Just... away.

"Hi," Mara heard herself bleat, waving in the most awkward manner possible. "Hi there, I'm Mara. Mara Matthews."

Perfection looked at her and beamed. "Oh my gosh, hi!" she twanged in the most perfect twang known to a Southern woman ever. "Josie Winchester. And you should hear the way Little Miss Hope goes on about you. She is just in heaven in this class. Me and her daddy will never get her to do anything else on a Saturday, so I hope you aren't thinking of ending this class ever."

Mara laughed awkwardly, but managed a smile for Hope. "Heh. No, no, I don't think I will be stopping soon, it's a nice break from my life. And um ..." She paused, clearing her throat. "I actually, uh ... I need to talk to you." She swallowed hard. "About Hope's dad."

Josie's brows lowered, and her perfect smile turned into a look of disgust. "Great." She looked in Hope's direction, blond ponytail tossing perfectly. "Hopey, what did your fool of a daddy do now?"

"How should I know?" Hope demanded in a voice too mature for her age.

Josie gave the little girl a hard look. "He's *your* daddy."

Hope propped a hand on her hip. "Well, he's *your* cousin."

Mara had been following the conversation like a tennis match, but now she froze from head to toe.

He was *what?*

"Oof," Josie said with a wince. "That's true. I have known him longer." She sighed and turned to Mara with an apologetic smile. "Whatever it is or was, I am so sorry on behalf of the entire family. Please don't judge me by my cousin."

Mara stared at her in amazement, struggling to form words. "Cousin?" she eventually managed. "You're his ... ?"

"Yes," Josie replied slowly, a wrinkle creasing her brow. Then it smoothed as her brows shot up, her eyes widened, and her jaw dropped. "Lawd have mercy ... You didn't ... you didn't think I was Z's trophy wife, did you?"

"Well, I ..."

"You did!" Josie overrode, her tone darkening. She turned to Hope with another dark look. "Hopey, that's it. I'm gonna kill your daddy."

"Not again ..." Hope groaned.

Josie shook her head, jaw visibly tightening. "If he would

get himself a girlfriend, or maybe even date, then I might actually get a date once in a while myself instead of being mistaken for that. Trophy wife. I can tell you, I would be an absolute trophy for whatever lucky man nabbed me." She huffed and sputtered through her lips. "I don't get paid enough for this."

Hope watched her father's cousin with wide eyes. "Josie-Jo, you're being crazy."

That seemed to break Josie out of her tirade, and she put a hand to her brow. "I know. I know, I'm sorry." She smiled for Mara again, and Perfection was back in place. "Sorry, Miss Mara. Now, what did you need to tell me about Zane?"

At the moment, she was rather inclined to sing praises and break into rather uncoordinated dance moves, if not pass out from being joyously lightheaded.

Thankfully, none of those things happened.

Mara shook her head with a kind smile instead of hugging this wonderful woman before her. "Nothing. Just wanted to remind him of the daddy-daughter day next week. I know he can be private, but I wanted to make sure he had the opportunity."

Josie flashed a quick grin. "Perfect. He'll be in town, so I'll make sure he knows. Hope would love to have him there, wouldn't you, hon?"

"Yeah!" Hope jumped up and down in her excitement, sending her pigtail braids bouncing again.

Mara had to laugh, and Josie did as well. "Come on, monkey. Your dad texted that he's going to run some quick errands, and then he'll meet us at home." She smiled at Mara with genuine warmth. "Nice to meet you officially, Mara."

"You too," Mara told her, hoping her relief at saying so wasn't completely obvious.

She watched as the two of them left the room, then released a very slow, almost steady breath.

*He is single.*

Not that it mattered all that much, as he would still have to find her attractive and interesting and a dozen other things for his relationship status to have any real effect on her life.

But he was *single.*

Single.

Holy crap, the man was single.

The man who had walked towards her and her parents last night with a warm smile, his leather jacket doing nothing to hide the utterly perfect fit of his T-shirt, and whose banter had made Mara dizzy with delight.

He was single.

It took a moment for her to realize her mouth was moving up and down, opening and closing like a fish. Well, she was pathetic, and that was all that could be said for her. She shut off the lights to the room and headed for the locker rooms, feeling the need for a shower.

Though she wasn't sure if it should be hot or cold.

Either. Both. First one, then the other.

As long as she was fast, it didn't matter all that much. It was cold enough outside to do the trick.

She hurried through showering and changing, then waved bye to the trainers, especially the ones indicating she should come lift with them.

Not today, not after this discovery.

She wanted to run out and get her hair done, get a manicure, get her teeth whitened, and buy an entirely new wardrobe. She didn't have the money to do any of those things, of course, so she would settle for the next-best things.

Chocolate and carbs.

Her car warmed up quickly, and the seat warmer was her best friend as she turned up the music to belt out whatever was on. It was stupid, and it was naive, but she suddenly felt more free than she had ever felt in her entire life. No more guilt, no more burden, no more reason to turn or look away.

She could look at Zane Winchester all she wanted and enjoy what she saw.

There was a thought for the ages.

Clearing her throat of its suddenly rather awkward lump, Mara pulled into the parking lot of the supermarket and quickly found a spot. The best place to get chocolate and carbs would be at the bakery, and she had every intention of doing so, but if she wanted to eat anything at her house later, she would need groceries. She gasped at the frigid air as she made her way to the store, and she hustled inside, releasing a satisfied exhale when she walked through the gust of heat in the entry.

She grabbed a basket and began to dart around the aisles, picking up what she could remember needing, wishing she had thought ahead enough to make a list. Still, aside from her insanely picky taste in bread, it shouldn't be too difficult to grab things she was sure she either needed now or would need shortly. That and visit the candy aisle, which would take up most of her time. The best candy shopping would come a few days after Valentine's Day, as everything would be on sale, but her supply was low now, and she would need to restock.

With a quick step, she headed down the next aisle, her attention focused on the peanut butter she was going to pick up in a very smooth motion without stopping, when a motion to her right caught her eye.

Just a guy reaching for a frozen pizza on the opposite side of the aisle—and she smiled ruefully at the stereotype.

Then he turned to put it in the cart, and Mara stopped dead in her tracks.

*Zane.*

She'd have to go by him to get her peanut butter, if she

really wanted it, and there was no way any smooth motion would be involved now.

No freaking way.

*He's single.*

Mara shushed her brain with a scowl. As if that statement would help anybody right now.

*Quick, act natural!*

She turned to her left and looked at the row of jams next to her, pretending she was actually seeing them and caring about what she saw. Cautiously, she took one step forward, then another, until a steady motion was reached and she didn't feel so robotic.

Just when she thought he might not notice her, and all of this would be for nothing, she heard his squeaking cart stop.

"Well, well, well. Of all the grocery stores in all the towns..."

Mara's smile was one of relief just as much as it was one of delight, but she tucked it back as she turned to look at the grinning facade of a very attractive man in a dark hoodie. "Hmm. We really need to stop meeting like this."

Zane lifted a brow. "What, on accident?"

"Uh-huh." Mara nodded, moving her basket from her arm to both hands, dangling it casually in front of her. "I might start thinking you're following me."

"You showed up at *my* game, Mara," he reminded her, his smile turning crooked. "I was there first."

"Maybe I liked the Hounds long before you played for them." She shrugged her shoulders, her smile getting harder to hide. "Accidental sighting still."

Zane nodded slowly, his lips pursing in thought while mischief danced in his eyes. "Well, I could always meet up with you on purpose. Save fate the trouble, keep my reputation free from the accusation of stalking."

Mara's heart screeched to the right side of her chest, held in place only by the now-bruised ribs. "You wouldn't want to do that. Might start something."

"It might," he agreed, nodding one more time. "I'm actually hoping it might."

Uhh, what?

The smile Mara had been fighting wavered against her cheeks. "Really?" she asked, her playful tone nowhere in sight. Only cold fear blended with hope remained.

"I did offer to take you out last night," he reminded her as he leaned against the handle of his cart. "With your parents, I might add, and I'd have happily entertained you all and made a good impression, if for no other reason than to prove a point."

"Wh-what point?"

Well, *that* wasn't a flirtatious response. Her face flamed at her complete awkwardness in front of him.

He saw it, his eyes darting to various parts of her face, his smile now tinged with something that made her toes bunch up in her tennis shoes.

"To be determined," Zane drawled. "Now, are you going to take me up on an intentional meeting? You already turned me down once. A second time, and I might think it's personal."

Mara swallowed hastily, desperate to regain some footing in this conversation. "Do you always take people out after your games just because you know them?"

"Only when I want to get to know them better," he retorted, completely unperturbed. "And only when I can't get them out of my head."

Whatever reply Mara had started to make vanished when he said that. She stared at him, filled with wonder on the inside while her outside, she was sure, displayed overt speculation and disbelief.

Not necessarily attractive, but real.

Hadn't he said he liked real?

Real she could handle.

"Yikes," she said without thinking, which was as real as she could get. "Me in your head." She hissed, making a face. "Sounds scary."

Zane chuckled softly, which did amazing things for his features. "So make it less scary. What do you say?"

It didn't seem polite to punch the air in victory or fall at his feet, but she definitely couldn't hold back her smile now. Instead, she let it spread as wide as it wanted to go, come what may.

"If you're going to insist, I suppose I'd better go along." She found herself shaking her head, her cheeks already aching, even as she tried to roll her eyes. "I was planning on going to the bakery after this for some cocoa and a pastry."

His eyes narrowed. "Your family's? Across the street?"

"That's the one," she confirmed. "Chocolate and carbs, if you will. If that's on your athletic diet, I'd be happy to have you meet me there on purpose."

The smile Zane gave her as he straightened did unspeakable things to the backs of her knees and up her thighs. "I don't care what's on my diet, Mara Matthews. Chocolate and carbs is perfect. It's a date. Meet you there in fifteen." He pushed his cart forward to continue his shopping, keeping his eyes on hers until he passed her.

If the burning along her spine was any indication, he kept looking at her as he moved away. She wouldn't look, couldn't look, as she continued down the aisle towards the peanut butter. Her shaking fingers reached for a jar, hefted it in her hand for a moment, and then her traitorous eyes slid back down the aisle towards the end.

Zane was still there, cart turned in the process of leaving the aisle, but stopped. And he was still looking at her. Smiling.

Mara smiled back, quirked her head in a show of a dare, and tapped an imaginary watch on her wrist.

Zane's smile spread, and he placed two fingers at his temple before dropping them in a salute. Then he pushed the cart out of her view and was gone.

Holy crap . . .

Mara bit her lip and screwed up her eyes on a high-pitched squeal, then raced out of the aisle, away from the direction Zane had gone, and headed for the registers, not caring that she hadn't gotten even half of the things she'd intended to.

She had a date in thirteen minutes, and no time to waste.

# SEVEN

THE BAKERY SMELLED heavenly as Zane entered, running a hand through his hair quickly before taking a hair tie and pulling it back. He didn't think Mara was the sort to care, but without product at hand, styling his hair wasn't an option, and leaving it down would make him look dingy.

He couldn't look dingy with Mara.

Something lurched in the center of his chest, and he swallowed in discomfort, one hand going to his sternum involuntarily.

Was he nervous? He hadn't felt like this in years, if ever, and he played hockey professionally. To be fair, out there he knew what he was doing, what to expect, and could move with confidence.

This was much worse.

He was completely out of his depth, and there was no way he could let Mara see that.

Chocolate and carbs, she'd said. Sounded simple enough.

One look around the place told him he didn't have to worry about meeting fans or reporters here. It was the most homey, cozy bakery he had ever been in, almost sleepy in its mood, despite being half full and the staff behind the counter and in the kitchen clearly bustling. The displays up front were incredible, mouthwatering for any dessert lover, carb lover, or flat-out food lover. Hope would have had her fingers and nose pressed to the glass in awe, and he'd have used that as an excuse to stand closer to it himself.

Pictures hung around the walls, mostly of family, friends, and famous people who had been in, though there were some classic Southern touches in the decor as well. One photo showed an entire collegiate team dressed in their travel warmups all giving thumbs-up to the camera while Mr. Matthews sat at the end of their table with a little girl on his knee.

A closer examination proved the little girl to be Mara, unless she had a sister who looked almost identical to her, but for the sparkle to the eyes, the hint of dimple in one cheek, and the dusting of freckles, though they were more prominent in the photo than they were now.

Zane smiled at seeing it, then allowed himself a brief exhale as he started further into the bakery. He glanced over at the counter, smiling politely at the teenager there, oddly grateful to not see Mara's parents.

He'd liked them well enough; he just didn't want them to know this was happening.

Yet.

His phone buzzed in his back pocket, and he pulled it out, glancing at the screen automatically. He smirked to see a string of texts in his group chat entitled The Pit, meaning his pals from his Northbrook Hockey Elite days were fired up about something. There was no telling what that could be.

*Clint: Z! That was a sick hit on McClaine!*

*Declan: I watched it like 5 times. Some serious air.*

*Rocco: I give it a 7. No twists.*

*Trane: It was a thing of beauty. Made highlight reels this AM, anyone catch those?*

*Jax: Nah, bro, the trick play in OT was the beauty. Gonna be studied in film all week, guaranteed.*

*Clint: I'm already practicing it.*

Zane shook his head, grinning to himself, and typed out a quick response.

*Zane: You'd have to practice, Fido, to even come close to making it work. Takes skill. BRB, got a meeting real quick.*

There was no way he was going to let them know what was really going on. He was the one who usually gave them grief about personal lives, and he knew full well he would be getting punishment back in full once word got out.

If it got out.

If this became something.

He slid his phone back into his jeans pocket and began to scan the room again, this time looking for a very particular brunette.

A smile flashed across his face as he saw her sitting in a corner booth drumming her fingers on the table. She'd redone her hair since the grocery store, and he thought he detected a sheen of lip gloss or balm on her lips. She didn't need it; he found her mouth distracting enough as it was.

At least she hadn't changed her clothes. There was something he loved about the black leggings and oversized gray sweater combo on her, something easy and laid back. Natural, even.

Real.

He kept coming back to that word, and it just seemed to fit. Mara was real.

But how real?

He headed towards the table, smiling when her attention fell on him, and thinking about what her quick, almost shy smile made him feel.

"Hey there," Zane greeted her, sliding his hands into his pockets. "This seat taken?"

Mara's smile spread for just a moment, and she shook her head. "No. Please, take it."

"Thank you, I will." He slid into the booth next to her and sighed as he settled in, looking at Mara and smiling. "Hi."

She snickered softly and propped her elbow on the table, her hand at the side of her head, looking at him. "Hi. Long time, no see."

"Cute." He scoffed and made a point of looking around the bakery, even though he'd made a study of it already. "This is nice. Really, this is a great place."

"You'd been here before, you said."

"I have." He returned his attention to her, crooked smile in place. "Drive-thru."

"Ah." Mara nodded in understanding. "Figures."

He chuckled at the gentle ribbing. "I'll have you know that Hope loves the drive-thru. Asks for it all the time. Better I bring her here than some fast food place."

Mara's eyes narrowed. "He says to the girl who happened upon him at the mall in the middle of a fast food meal . . ."

"Okay," he protested, giving her a look. "Just take the compliment, will you? We'll discuss my potentially terrible meal tendencies another time."

"I'll pencil it in," she quipped. She smiled again, then raised her head and looked around. "No, you're right, it's nice. I tend to forget that, since I've grown up here. Every day after school, any time I was home from college, we were here. I was working here."

Zane made a low sound of acknowledgement. "It's surprising you didn't go into business, then. Or baking."

Mara's mouth curved to one side. "Oh, trust me, the pressure was there. And I know my way around the kitchen, but I didn't want to be stuck here forever. I mean . . ." She rolled her eyes, laughing at herself. "Here I am anyway, but my job is my own, and so is my life."

"And your folks were okay with that?"

She nodded, her eyes coming back to him. "Yeah. I think the pressure I was feeling was more of what I *thought* they wanted than what they *actually* wanted. I did it to myself. And anyway, my brother and his wife want to take over. Heaven help us when they do, Ashley is terrible in the kitchen."

Her expression made Zane laugh, and he would have pressed her on that, had a teenage waiter not appeared at the table.

"You guys ready to order yet?" he asked, grinning between the two of them in the polite manner every waiter is trained on. "Hey, Mars."

Mara gave him a tiny wave. "Hey, Chip. Cocoa and *pain au chocolat*."

Chip nodded before turning his attention to Zane. His eyes widened, recognition dawning. "And for you?" he asked faintly.

Zane glanced down at the menu on the table. "Coffee, black, and a berry-berry scone."

"Coming up," Chip said quickly before dashing off, bumping into a table in his hurry.

"Wow," Mara commented dryly as she watched him go. She turned to Zane with a quizzical look. "Does that happen often?"

Sensing he was being teased more than genuinely asked, he only shrugged and made a face.

She laughed and sat back against the booth. "What it must be like to be a big shot."

Now his face contorted into one of distaste, which made Mara laugh more. He liked that laugh, he decided. It wasn't giggly or bright, it didn't squeak or squeal, and it was fairly infectious. And well used.

Mara laughed a lot.

With a laugh like that, he would too.

"Not all it's cut out to be," he assured Mara on an exhale. "Everything you say or do is captured and discussed, and people expect you to be larger than life."

Mara gave him a wry look. "I've seen you play. You *are* larger than life."

He looked down at the table, tapping his finger on the top absently. "On the ice, maybe. Off the ice, I'm just me. Still the scrawny late bloomer from Chicago just trying to keep up."

"Scrawny?" Mara tilted her head back to laugh once. "No way. Not that build."

Zane smirked and raised a brow. "You noticed, huh?"

Her face flamed, and she clamped down on her lips hard. "Might have . . ."

"Hesitation and . . . guilt?" he prodded. He leaned closer, giving her a friendly wink. "Don't worry, Josie lit into me before I got here. I know you thought we were married."

"Oh, good," Mara groaned, putting her face into her hands. "This just gets better and better."

Zane chuckled and scooted closer, rubbing a soothing hand on her back. "Oh, stop, I'm just giving you a hard time. It's my own fault, I rely on Josie way too much. It's too easy having a cousin as the nanny."

Mara dropped her hands and folded her arms on the table, cheeks still bright, and looked at him. "Nanny? I wouldn't have pegged her for that."

"She's pretty much the stand-in mom for Hope," he told her bluntly. "When I got picked up by Tennessee, she was the first call I got. Insisted that I let her help with Hope, since she lived here, and when I'm on extended trips, my aunt and uncle host Hope for sleepovers."

"How does she manage that, though?" Mara asked, her brow creasing. "Is Hope her full-time job?"

It was a fair question, but it made Zane laugh anyway. "No, although with Hope, you never know. Josie is a graphic artist, so she does most of her work on the computer. AKA she can work from home."

"And home is . . . ?"

"Sometimes with us at our house," Zane allowed. "She has a room there, of course. She also has her own place. With my in-season schedule, I don't know how I would manage without her."

Mara hummed a short, noncommittal sound. "Well, now that I know who she is, I can honestly say that I like her."

That was an interesting way of putting it, and Zane leaned back a touch, considering Mara in all her glory. "So you didn't like her before you knew who she was?"

Her blue eyes widened, and she wrenched her gaze away. "Okay, moving on. New topic."

"And what should that be?" Zane wondered aloud, his hand slowly moving along Mara's back again. He felt her shiver beneath his hand, and the sensation rippled up his arm and into his chest.

Mara gnawed on her lower lip for a moment, sending a jolt of awareness into Zane's stomach. "You were scrawny, you said. So how'd a scrawny kid wind up being an animal on the ice?"

Zane sat back once more, thinking back with a nostalgic smile. "Self-preservation. Pure and simple. I'm from Chicago, and there's a hockey program there, Northbrook."

"I saw the write-up about that gala in November," Mara murmured, not looking at him. "And the all-star game last month."

Had she been looking him up? That was the only way he

could think she would know about those things. Big news though they were, it wasn't much outside of the sports world.

Mara had looked him up. Why did that make him satisfied somehow?

"Yep, those were for fundraising there," he went on, letting the point go. "It's in trouble now, but back in its day, it was huge. Best team in the nation, and I'm not just saying that; we took titles on a regular basis. I had skills on the ice, but I wasn't big enough to be much of a threat. One day, I got tired of getting pushed around, and I decided to use my body as much as I used my head."

"Um, ouch."

Zane chuckled. "Not so ouch then, but it made a point. I gave everything I had in every play. Every minute of every game or practice, I was in it. Had to be, if I wanted to stick around. Made myself a force to be reckoned with, small as I was. Then I grew, and . . ."

Mara did look at him now, somehow amused by something he had said. "And the habit stuck."

He met her eyes squarely. "Guess so. No sense going backwards, right?"

Slowly she shook her head. "No sense."

His hand continued to move along her back, and that connection was suddenly powerful, the touch of fabric against his skin electrifying, and he would swear he could feel the beat of her heart through it.

But her eyes . . . He couldn't look away from them, his mind shuffling through various things to compare their shade to and coming up short. They were amazing, though, in a way that reminded him of this bakery.

It felt like home.

And that was terrifying.

"Cocoa for Mara," Chip said, announcing his presence with perfect timing.

Zane scooted back to his original place in the booth, clearing his throat. Then he saw the massive mug of hot chocolate and gaped. "Now wait a minute..."

"Too late!" Mara crowed in victory, taking the mug from Chip. "No take-backs."

"And coffee for you, sir," Chip told him, a laugh in his voice as the usual-sized mug of coffee was set before him.

Zane looked at the differences, then up at Mara. "This is so not fair."

She shrugged and lifted her cocoa to her lips, sipping loudly before sighing dramatically. "Too bad, so sad."

"You're loving this."

"Oh yeah, I really am." She grinned brightly, then looked at Chip. "Thanks, pal. How long for the pastries?"

Chip nodded at her. "Coming right up." He turned and left them, this time at a normal pace and without hitting the table.

Zane heaved a noisy exhale and shook his head at Mara. "You did that on purpose, Mara."

"I did not," she retorted. "I would never dictate what you should get. It's not my fault you missed the massive hint when I said chocolate and carbs..."

"Unbelievable." He groaned playfully and made a face as he took a sip of his comparatively pathetic-sized coffee. "At least the coffee is good."

Mara's brows rose. "I'll have you know everything is good here."

On cue, Chip brought their pastries and set them before them. "Here you go, guys. Enjoy!" He turned to go, then spun back around. "Hey, Mars, that work drama cleared up yet?"

Mara's expression completely changed, and Zane watched it with interest. "No," Mara all but growled. "I don't think it will, so I'll just deal with it."

"Sorry," Chip said with a click of his tongue. "You could always quit and come back here!"

"Funny, Chip," Mara told him with full sarcasm in force. "Really, so funny. Table twelve wants you. Bye now."

Chip held up his hands in a helpless gesture, spinning around and heading towards the table she'd indicated.

"So that's what you get from your dad," Zane commented in the most offhand way he could manage while grinning.

Mara's eyes flicked to him. "What?"

He lifted one shoulder, halfway to a shrug without fully committing. "I heard the exact same tone from your dad last night. It's funny, actually."

"You're not laughing," she pointed out.

"I'm curious about what he said," Zane told her. "'Work drama.' Your entire body language changed when he said that. Everything okay?"

He could see Mara stiffening before him, and he didn't like it one bit.

"No," she said flatly, averting her eyes. "But it's fine. We all have our things, right?"

She didn't want to talk about it, that much was clear, but it was also clear that things were not fine. He wanted to know what it was, and more than that, he wanted to make it right.

Now wasn't the time. But if he had his way, played his cards right, maybe the time would come.

Maybe.

"Right," he murmured, digging into his scone without paying much attention. He paused as he really tasted it, and he moaned almost exactly the way Mara had with her burger at the mall. "Oh my gosh . . ."

Mara burst out laughing, a hint of chocolate at the corner of her mouth from her own pastry. "What did I say?"

"I will never doubt you again," he groaned as he took another bite, this one much bigger.

She grinned and ran her thumb along the side of her mouth, capturing the chocolate there. "Dang straight, Zane."

He paused again, this time looking at her with more intensity than he usually spared off of the ice.

She stilled. "What?"

"You've never called me Zane," he told her in a low voice, feeling the rumble of it more than the sound. "Ever."

"Sure I have," she scoffed with a wave of her hand.

He shook his head firmly. "No. You haven't. You haven't called me anything."

Her eyes went round. "Oh." She swallowed once, and his eyes darted to the movement of her throat. "And?"

He dragged his eyes back up to hers, heat coiling within him. "I like it. A lot."

Mara exhaled, and he wished to heaven he could translate the sound. "Okay," she murmured.

Zane smiled slightly and nodded back. "Okay." His phone buzzed in his pocket, and he ignored it, going back in for more of his scone.

"Get it," Mara told him.

He looked up at her. "What?"

"Your phone," she clarified. "I heard it buzz. Get it. It's fine."

She was generous, but he knew it was probably The Pit being obnoxious. "No, really . . ."

She gave him a hard look, which he was learning she was quite good at. "It could be Hope. You get a pass on the checking-your-phone thing. Get it, or I'll come over there and do it."

Zane quirked his brows at her. "That sounds like a more interesting idea."

"Zane . . ." Mara scolded like she might have done with Chip.

He laughed and pulled his phone out. "Fine, fine." He glanced at the screen, then frowned. "Crap."

"What?"

He met Mara's eyes with a sigh. "Josie. I forgot she has a hair appointment, and she is demanding I come home so she isn't late. I neglected to tell her I was coming here with you." He grimaced, looking down at their half-eaten scones. "This isn't how I imagined this going."

Mara waved a hand again. "It's fine! Absolutely fine, no worries whatsoever, I'll just . . ."

His phone buzzed in his palm, and he glanced down, fully scowling now.

"Oh dear. More?"

"Valentines," he grumbled, shaking his head. "We have to do valentines today."

"Well, yeah," Mara said in confusion. "That is this coming week. You should have picked up a box at the store."

He shook his head again. "Hope wants to *make* valentines. Josie's bowing out, the traitor, and I have zero artistic ability or desire. Oy, this is bad." He squeezed his eyes shut and put his phone to his head.

"I could help."

His eyes sprang open, and he looked up at Mara. "What?"

She gestured lightly, her face clear of irony or suggestion. "I could help. Arts and crafts with a five-year-old sounds like a riot. I'll just come to your house and crank a few out, good to go, problem solved."

Zane blinked at her. "You're serious."

Her hands gestured in a much more sarcastic way this time. "Duh. Let's go." She slid out of the booth, grabbing her pastry in one hand. "I mean it, let's go, Daddy-o. I've seen Josie irritated. Do you want to see that tomorrow?"

He laughed at that, unable to believe this woman had not

only met him here but was now demanding he get up so she could come home with him. To help his daughter make valentines.

If he hadn't been hooked on her before, he was getting there now.

He grinned up at her and made his way out of the booth, reaching for his leftover scone as he did so. "Fine. You'll follow me there?"

Mara smirked at him. "I might have cyber-stalked you, Zane Winchester, but I didn't physically stalk you. Yes, I'm following you."

"So you *did* look me up. Well, well, well . . ." He folded his arms, daring her to refute it.

"Heck yeah, I did," she shot back, completely unfazed. "And the photos don't begin to do you justice." She quirked her brows and strode for the door.

Zane grinned after her, laughing for no reason whatsoever.

Yep. He was hooked.

So, so hooked.

# EIGHT

"It's okay, it's fine. It's fine. You just invited yourself to Zane Winchester's house. For arts and crafts."

She sighed loudly and shook her head. "You idiot."

There was really no other word for it. She hadn't even been thinking when she'd suggested it; it had just seemed the logical thing to do. He didn't want to make them—would probably butcher them—and it would crush a creative girl like Hope to not have the exact valentines she wanted. He would have given his all to the effort, but ultimately, it wouldn't have been a great outcome.

Artistically speaking.

Not that the art was the most important thing, but it did help.

Mara could help there.

But it was *Zane*. She had invited herself over to *his* house.

If their brief date at the bakery was any indication, she'd embarrass herself twelve more times and catch on fire at least three.

And yet . . .

He actually seemed interested in her. He stared at her a

little too long, asked questions with too much interest, and teased her a little too freely. She knew she was shamelessly staring at times and that her quips were a little too frequent, but she was used to saying things without thinking.

Hence the driving to his house for valentine making.

She shook her head on an exhale as she followed his SUV into a neighborhood, expecting to see grand houses with gated driveways.

This was not that kind of neighborhood.

The houses were moderately sized, clean and well-kept but hardly luxury. They all had either a traditional farmhouse look or more of a plantation style, but they all blended together seamlessly. Some were older than others and some had clearly been redone, but all in all, it was a classic neighborhood that had been around for a while. More than that, there were people milling about in their yards, kids bundled up and running around, and a few people out on walks with their dogs.

This was where a hockey superstar lived?

Zane pulled his SUV into the driveway of an older yet renovated home, the facade a perfect blend of the styles she'd seen. The second-story terrace in the center called to Mara's more Southern roots and tastes.

She'd have taken a mug of cocoa and a rocker up to that terrace and stayed for hours looking at the stars.

What would Zane think of that?

She shook her head and pulled into the drive behind Zane, turning off the car and gripping the steering wheel for a moment.

"You're crazy, Mara June," she told herself, sounding very much like her father when she did so.

That made her frown.

"Shut your piehole," she muttered as she clambered out of the car, fidgeting with her hair as nerves washed over her.

Zane was waiting for her in the garage, smiling in invitation but seeming to let her have a moment.

Great.

She covered by looking up and around at the house, nodding in approval. "Subtle, tasteful, and classic."

"Thank you, I do try."

Mara blinked and looked at him dryly. "The house, Zane."

He shrugged, his eyes widening innocently. "What did you think I meant?"

Now Mara rolled her eyes and came over to him. "Incorrigible."

"How can a house be incorrigible?" he asked, turning to lead her into the house.

Without thinking, she slapped him on the back. "You, genius!"

He laughed in protest and darted forward, away from her. "Oh, I'm sorry. I get so confused."

"Clearly." She huffed in faux irritation but couldn't help grinning. Zane's playful side was definitely an attractive one.

Not that he had an unattractive side.

She'd have to rank his various sides by attractiveness sometime, just for organization's sake.

Zane didn't even pause at the door to the house, pushing it open as though it were completely normal for him to bring a random woman over to the house.

Oh gosh, what if this was normal?

Her toe caught the edge of the threshold of the door, and she barely caught herself on the frame before she actually stumbled into his house. Which would be perfect, because then she could turn and run out to her car for an escape.

But that would also require her to fall flat on her face in front of Zane, which would pretty much be death.

"Hello?" Zane called out as he strode into the kitchen, apparently missing Mara's almost disastrous moment. "Where's the chaos that was threatened?"

"Oh, it's coming, buddy!" a familiar voice rang out, twang in full force. "You have no idea how lucky you are."

Mara winced as she moved fully into the kitchen, the warm off-yellow color of the walls offsetting the antique-looking white cabinets in a perfect way, though it would clash with her blush horribly.

Figures.

Josie was grabbing her tan slouchy purse from the table while shrugging into a burgundy fleece, her attention entirely focused on getting out the door. "Hope's had an early lunch, and everything you'll need for valentines is in her cubby. I donated a shoebox for the efforts, it's on the stairs. Don't do anything about dinner, Mama's bringing chili."

Mara bit her lip as she slowly, casually made her way to the massive island in the kitchen, resting her hands on it, waiting for the reaction she might fear most.

Josie looked up then, digging for her keys in her purse. She stopped, her eyes flicking from Mara to Zane and back again. A small smile lit her lips, and she removed her hand from her purse, pointing between them. "Oh . . . oh, I like this. Yeah. Yeah, this is good." She nodded repeatedly as she came around the table and went by Zane to grab a bottle of water from a minifridge on the counter.

Patting Zane on the shoulder, Josie nodded again to herself, sighing as if in relief. She smiled at Mara and reached out a hand to pat the top of hers. "Hey, Mara. Nice to see you again."

Mara swallowed with difficulty, her throat completely parched. "Hi, Josie."

Josie winked, then moved past her for the door, whistling

a song to herself that Mara could still hear echoing in the garage when the door was closed.

"Right," Zane said slowly in the suddenly awkward space. "So that's Josie."

"Yeah," Mara replied. She nodded shakily, tension spreading across her neck and shoulders. "Yeah, I know."

They shared a strained smile that reflected the awkwardness Mara felt curling in her stomach.

Zane suddenly cleared his throat before calling, "Hope! Hopey-Dope, where art thou?"

"Coming!" a cheery little voice shouted as a series of pattering thumps sounded from above them.

"Where art thou?" Mara repeated with a wry look.

He returned the look without shame. "She's my princess, so . . ."

She couldn't argue with that, and she smiled without really meaning to. "That's sweet."

Zane smiled back, ruefully this time. "I was kidding . . . but if you like that, I'll keep it up."

"I should have known," she muttered. "Are you ever serious, Zane Winchester?"

"Oh yeah." He leaned on the island, a swagger of sorts entering his frame. "When it matters most, I am as serious as they come."

Shivers tingled at the base of Mara's spine, but she refused to give in to the sensation. She placed her hands on the countertop herself and leaned towards him, eyes narrowing. "I'll believe it when I see it," she whispered.

Zane lowered himself to resting on his elbows, bringing his face closer to hers. "Is that a challenge, Miss Matthews? I can assure you, I have a very, very long history of owning every single challenge thrown down in front of me."

The shivers were going to ripple across her entire body

soon, but she wasn't going to let him know that her knees were already shaking. "Sure," she managed to say, keeping her voice low. "If you want it to be."

"Oh, I think I do want," he murmured with a very slow smile. "And I think you do too."

Well, the shivers burst into flames at that, scorching everything from the tips of her toes to the ends of her hair.

"Do I?" she asked of no one at all, her voice still low, her eyes on his.

Yes, she did.

*Hells* yes she did; the fire said so, and her breathlessness echoed that.

If Zane's smile was any indication, he saw that in her face at this moment.

Whoops.

"Daddy, is it time for valentines now?" Hope asked as she darted down the stairs.

Zane straightened away from Mara, almost jerking to face his daughter. "Guess so, pumpkin. First you need to say hi to someone."

Hope looked at Mara and gasped. "Miss Mara! You came over to my house!"

There was nothing to do except grin at her for that. Mara pushed back from the counter, hands on her hips. "I sure did! How about you give me a tour?"

"Yes!" Hope dashed over to her and took her hand, tugging her out of the large kitchen, through some french doors, into a dining room. The house was arranged in a formal layout, but the atmosphere was so relaxed it was hard to think of it as anything but comfortable.

"This is the fancy room," Hope told Mara in an important voice. "We *never* eat in here unless it's Christmas, Thanksgiving, or a birthday. Or if lots of the family is here.

Aunt Penny loves to eat in here when she comes. Josie says it's cuz she's pretendous."

Zane coughed a startled laugh behind them. "Pretentious, sweetheart?"

"Pretendous, yeah," Hope replied. She returned her attention to the room. "And over there is my piano!"

Mara looked, and sure enough, an old but utterly classic piano sat tucked in a corner, framed photos across the entire top. "Are you a musician, Hope?"

"Yep!" She nodded happily, pulling Mara over to the instrument. "Daddy says I can start taking lessons when I'm six. Claire's mommy will teach me, and we've had that piano my whole life and no one can play it except Gramma Annie." She pointed at a picture of an older woman pushing her in a swing.

"She looks so fun!" Mara told her, smiling. She looked at the rest of the pictures, her brow furrowing as she saw more grandparents and a ton of adults and other kids.

Was this all family? It was huge!

And which of these were Hope's mom? Or were any of them?

"Grandpa Charlie can play too, baby," Zane reminded her softly from behind them.

Mara glanced back at him, seeing him leaning against the french doors, hands in his pockets, a smile on his lips. "Your dad?"

His eyes flicked to her, the smile tightening. "No."

And that was all he said.

Hope tugged on Mara's sleeve. "Grandpa Charlie is my extra grandpa, Miss Mara. I'm that special, I get an extra."

Mara smiled at her and ran a hand over her hair. "You are so lucky. What other rooms do you have, huh?"

Again, she was tugged along, this time to the foyer,

though just in passing on the way to the next room, which was locked.

"This is Daddy's exercise room," Hope told her in a very serious tone. "I can't go in there without a grown-up."

"Seems wise." Mara nodded in approval. "We have that rule at the gym, don't we?"

"It's a good rule," Zane pointed out.

Hope was already moving on, pulling her down a hallway off the main portion of the house. "This is Josie's room, and her bathroom."

"Let's not go down there, Hopey," Zane called, a smile in his voice. "Mara doesn't need to see that. How about the TV room?"

"Okay!" Almost spinning on her heel, Hope changed direction and yanked Mara's arm to follow.

Mara looked at Zane as she passed him. "You're enjoying this, aren't you?"

He nodded with a cheeky grin. "So much."

"Jerk."

He dipped his chin in acknowledgement. "Thank you."

"This is the bestest room *ever*, Miss Mara," Hope assured her as they entered. "Look!"

Mara's eyes went wide as she took it in, and she was inclined to agree. One wall was almost ceiling to floor windows with an incredible view of a backyard and tons of trees in the distance. In the fall, it must be breathtaking.

A huge sectional took up most of the room, with a massive flat-screen TV on the wall opposite, just above a stone fireplace, shelves of movies on either side. Pictures of family decorated the other remaining wall, a montage of laughter, love, and apparently chaos. Some stunning beauties in the family—and she recognized Zane in a number of them. For such a private guy, there were a lot of pictures everywhere.

Interesting.

"This is the blanket closet, Miss Mara." Hope released her hand and darted over to a door next to the photos. She opened it wide and gestured grandly to shelves of blankets. "Just *look*!"

Mara grinned as she came over: patchwork quilts, fleece-tie blankets, and some Sherpa throws almost filled the entire thing. "That is amazing! How do you pick one?"

Hope giggled and pointed at a blue-and-purple patchwork quilt. "This one's my favorite."

"I like that one too," Mara told her with a wink. "Where did you get it?"

"Grandma Rae and Papa Tom," she reported proudly. "And this one is from Gramma Annie and Papa Wayne. That one came from Aunt Julie, this one is from Uncle Kyle and Aunt Reeree . . ."

Mara was beginning to get dizzy with names, and she was relieved when she heard Zane.

"Hope, Mara is going to help you with valentines," he interrupted with the gentle firmness of a father. "Why don't you go get what you need from your Imagination Station?"

Hope beamed and skipped away. "Okay! You can sit at the kitchen table, Miss Mara. I'll be right back!"

"Yes, ma'am." Mara smiled as she watched Hope high-five her dad as she passed him, then charge up the stairs.

"Sorry," Zane said softly, coming over to Mara. "She's a bit of a ham with guests."

Mara raised a brow. "Don't apologize for her excitement. I love it. Super cute, and it'll serve her well later."

Zane didn't look convinced, but his easy smile showed his true feelings. He looked at the wall of pictures, exhaling to himself. "I have a big family."

"Okay . . ." Mara came to his side and faced the wall with him. "I got that."

He laughed beside her. "No, I mean it's huge. My parents divorced when I was six."

Something cold swirled in Mara's chest as she looked at him. "Oh gosh, I'm so sorry."

To her surprise, he smiled. "Don't be. My parents parted on good terms. The marriage ended, but their friendship didn't. Look." He pointed at a picture of a middle-aged man walking a middle-aged woman down the aisle, both laughing. "That's my mom's wedding to Wayne. Dad gave her away."

"You're kidding." Mara moved closer to the picture, wanting a better look. Sure enough, between the two of them, she saw everything that would add up to Zane in appearance. "That's incredible."

"My parents co-parented my sisters and me," Zane told her, tapping at another picture. "In every sense of the term. We were together for everything. We may have rotated houses, but we were all a family. Everyone was at my hockey games. Everyone went to Alexa's soccer games. Everyone was there when Kerri was the lead in the high school musical. Instead of two families, we had one huge one."

Mara couldn't help but smile at the warmth in his tone as he spoke about his family. It was the same tone he had for Hope, and it just wrapped her up like one of the quilts in the closet. "How huge?"

Zane chuckled and gestured at one more picture, this one looking more like a mob. "Eight kids in all. Wayne had two, and Rae, my stepmom, had two. Then Dad and Rae had Logan, and that wrapped things up pretty good."

"Are you close with them?"

"Oh yeah. We're all close. Look." He plucked a picture off the wall and held it out to show her. "Alexa's wedding, three summers ago. Dad and Wayne both walked her down the aisle." He shook his head, grinning at some memory. "My uncle Ted gave a prayer before the dinner. Dad's brother. At the end of it, he shouted out something about getting an amen from the back, and all of my cousins and siblings shouted amen back."

Mara snickered, taking the picture from him. "That's hilarious."

"What's hilarious," Zane told her, "is that my stepsister Kaylee asked him to give the blessing at her wedding the next fall."

"So?"

Zane met her eyes, laughter dancing there. "Kaylee is Wayne's daughter. No relation to Uncle Ted. At all."

Mara shook her head in disbelief, grinning at what she saw in Zane's expression and the image he was painting in her mind. "That is amazing. Did he do it?"

"Of course. He's the family prayer-giver at all important events now." Zane looked back at the photos, and she detected some nostalgia in his gaze. "Divorce tears some families apart. But in my case, it made my family bigger. Better. I respect my parents a lot for that. Especially now."

That piqued Mara's interest. "Now?" she prodded hesitantly, wondering if he would open up. It was probably too soon. Had to be too soon. They barely knew each other, after all, and a few hours of flirting wasn't anything at all, really.

It was nothing.

"I got divorced five years ago," Zane said without looking at her. "Hope's mom . . . Michelle. She decided this life wasn't for her. Wanted out. I thought we could do everything like my parents did, wasn't worried about it. I'd seen it done, so I knew it could be done. I knew my parents were the exception in that department, but I wanted to try."

Dread and guilt prickled at Mara's neck and in the soles

of her feet. She scrunched her toes in an attempt to alleviate the feeling. "What happened?"

A bitter smile crossed Zane's lips, and he turned to face Mara directly. "She didn't want to co-parent. She didn't really want to parent at all. I have full custody of Hope, but Michelle can have any holiday she wants, and four weeks every summer. She's barely asked for any of it. I realize the actual divorce could have been uglier, but I didn't expect it to feel so cold."

Understanding began to dawn, and Mara's eyes widened. "So when Hope said she never gets to shop for a mom . . ."

Zane nodded once. "She was being literal. We call on important dates and when Hope asks to, but it's rare that Michelle picks up."

"And Grandpa Charlie?"

"Michelle's dad," Zane rasped, swallowing hard. "Great guy. Amazing guy, really. He came to me two years ago and asked if he could be in Hope's life again, even if Michelle didn't want to be. I was hesitant, but who am I to take Hope away from her family? Turns out, he's one of her favorite people on earth." He stepped closer to Mara, his eyes turning warmer despite the solemnity of the discussion. "She has no idea he's her mother's father. It kills me to do that, but after everything, that's what Charlie wants. And might even be what's best for Hope. And I have to think of what's best for her in everything now."

"So you're not looking for your next relationship to end in divorce, I'm guessing," Mara said without thinking.

Zane's eyes flashed, and he took a step closer to her. "Absolutely not."

Mara exhaled slowly, unable to take her eyes off of Zane's. How could she be so attracted to him when he was talking about such a sad situation? How could he be so calm and matter-of-fact? How could he be looking at *her* that way when she was asking so many personal questions?

"Sorry," Mara whispered as her cheeks flamed in delayed response. "It's none of my business."

"I don't care," he whispered back. "I don't mind sharing any of this with you. You thought I was married until this morning. If I'd known that the first time I met you, I would have said something. I'm not married, but I have been married. I haven't dated anyone seriously since then. Never found someone worth spending my time on, let alone Hope's."

Mara's breath stuttered in her chest, her lungs almost cramping with anticipation as hordes of butterflies took flight in her stomach.

"I'm not a player," he went on, still whispering, "and I'm not casual. Hope is everything. My family is everything. You asked me about serious, here it is: I take any and all relationships seriously. In this, I am the same on the ice and off. When I'm in, I'm all in. All in, all intense, all the way. All heart."

"Why are you telling me all this?" Mara managed to force out, her voice catching at least twice.

The corner of his mouth quirked in an almost smile, and he reached out to touch the braid across her brow. "Because I don't like that you woke up this morning thinking I wasn't interested. Or available. I want this to be your business, Mara. I want to be your business."

"You can't," she squeaked, shivering released in full force at the touch of his fingers against her hair. "You barely know me."

"I know." His smile spread, and something about it made Mara smile too. "So time for you to fix that. What do you do for fun, Mara?"

Fun? What was fun? Did she do fun things?

*Snap out of it; the beautiful man asked you a question!*

Mara blinked, wondering if her smile was as loopy as it felt. She forced herself to focus, blinking again. "Give me space to breathe or think," she told him, "and I might remember."

Zane's eyes widened, and then he threw his head back on a laugh. "Oh, Mara, that was amazing."

"What?" she demanded, laughing as she took a measured step back. "I'm a red-blooded female, and you smell insanely good, for one, and thinking goes to the backburner."

His smile turned ticklish, and he slid his hands safely into his hoodie pockets. "Fair enough. Distance. Better?"

"Better." She cleared her throat and smiled politely. "Fun. Bake, although that's practically a chore, so it's only fun sometimes. I do play volleyball on Monday nights."

"Oh yeah?" He lit up at that, the ticklish heat fading, thank goodness. "Like in a club?"

Mara shook her head. "Nothing that formal. Just a bunch of has-beens and wannabes playing around. The community center has courts open until nine, so we just head there."

"Interesting . . ." Zane mused, looking her up and down. "Volleyball. I can see that."

"Come on, Miss Mara!" Hope called, coming down the stairs at the perfect time. "We have *so* much work to do! Daddy won't help; he *hates* Valentine's Day."

Mara gave Zane a curious look as she started for the kitchen. "Does he? Interesting."

He made a face, shrugging his broad shoulders. "Guilty. Least favorite holiday of all time. Not a fan."

"Hmm" was all Mara said as she continued on, pulling out a kitchen chair and sitting down at the table as Hope laid out all of their supplies.

"What?" Zane followed them in, leaning against the stair railing. "What's 'hmm' supposed to mean?"

Mara took a leaf out of his book and shrugged. "The man who's all heart doesn't like the holiday of hearts. Interesting."

He lowered his chin to give her a more direct look. "I don't need a holiday of hearts to have one, Mara. Promise."

She could see that—had seen that—and she was beginning to feel that. Still, it was something she would tuck away in the back of her mind to ask about later.

Maybe.

She turned her attention to Hope and the task before them. "Right. Okay, kiddo, I love Valentine's Day, so we got this. Let me show you how to make lacy hearts."

# NINE

"You're out of your mind."

"No, I'm not. I'm being social. You always say I need to be more social."

Josie gave Zane a derisive look that only someone related to him would give. "Risking your body is not what I had in mind."

Zane frowned at her, lacing up his shoes. "I'm not risking my body, Jos."

"No? This from the guy who almost cried when his team played dodgeball against the Cougars for the Northbrook Challenge, because it could hurt him?" She snorted and went back to mixing cookie dough. "Boy, you are three kinds of stupid, and only one of them is okay."

"And which one is that?" he asked, knowing the answer would more than likely be ridiculous.

"The one where you're tripping over yourself for Mara. That's an acceptable and even cute stupid." She gestured at him with her dough-covered spoon. "This is the just-plain-dumb kind of stupid."

"What's the third?"

Josie glared at him. "I do not have time to list all the ways you are stupid."

Zane grinned. "You said three, so there's gotta be a specific one you're thinking of."

His cousin huffed, stirring the dough with more energy. "How about provoking me? That's really stupid, and you know it."

He pretended to think about that, then shook his head. "Nah, that's not it."

The stirring stopped, and she gave him a death-by-evil glare. "Inserting your size-thirteen foot into your piehole of a mouth. That's your special kind of stupid."

Sometimes he really adored his cousin. Zane shrugged one shoulder. "Well, we all have our strengths."

Josie sighed in irritation but cracked a smile. "So help me, Zane Thomas Winchester, I will intentionally put salmonella in your cookie dough one of these days."

The threat made him laugh, and he pushed up to his feet. "With this body? I wouldn't feel a thing." He pounded his stomach. "All iron, Jos."

"I'd like to take an iron to you." She shook her head and looked at the clock. "Better get going. You said it closes at nine. I'll stay over tonight, so you kids have fun as late as you want."

Zane came over to her, swiped a fingerful of cookie dough, and planted a noisy kiss on her cheek. "You are the best, Josie-Jo. I love you."

She wiped her cheek off and smacked his back with her free hand. "You better, mister. Tell Mara hi."

He chuckled and waved, heading out to the garage and his car, excitement bubbling up within him.

It was strange, feeling so much so fast, but it was also as natural a progression of feeling as he could ever remember having in his life. Mara was all warmth and fun, natural and comfortable and easy. Spending pretty much all day Saturday with her had been amazing, and it seemed like he had known her forever now. He'd had an away game yesterday, but Cleveland was an easy jaunt, so he wasn't in any way tired from that.

He'd been texting Mara almost the entire time he was away. There was nothing like finishing a game and finding a congratulatory text from her, and his stupid grin had taken ages to go away.

Boomer had monitored the entire thing out loud for him.

Zane had given him a couple of good body checks in practice today in retaliation. Boomer was a tough player and would give as good as he got, but he wasn't as intense as Zane.

No one was.

That was the point.

He hadn't seen Mara today, given his schedule and her schedule, and they didn't have any plans set for the week. He couldn't wait until they decided on something, so he was being impulsive and inviting himself to something he probably shouldn't be doing.

Recreational volleyball.

He loved the sport, played with his siblings and step-siblings at family gatherings, but he was usually pretty strict about additional physical activities during the hockey season. No sense in injuring himself, or risking injury, over something that wasn't even related to his sport. If his coaches knew what he was about to do, they wouldn't necessarily get after him, but they definitely would raise some eyebrows.

He wouldn't blame them.

But he also didn't have any reservations.

He wanted to be with Mara, and he wanted to prove that he could be part of her life as much as he wanted her to be part of his.

Might not make much sense, but there it was.

His car's Bluetooth suddenly signaled an incoming call, and he glanced at the dash quickly.

Bree Stone was calling. Interesting.

Bree was Clint McCarthy's better half, and she had decided to take on the impossible task of saving the Northbrook Hockey program. He'd gone to her gala in November, helped with camps when he could, and played in a promo all-star game she'd spearheaded. Now her new nonprofit, Prime Outreach Incorporated, was digging into the deeper stuff. It had been a minute since she'd reached out about another opportunity, but he found himself smiling at the thought of more ideas on her end.

She hadn't had a bad one yet.

Except maybe falling for Clint, but there was no accounting for taste.

He hit the answer button. "Z here."

"Hey Zane!" Her voice chimed with a brightness she didn't usually possess. "How are things?"

"Warm and sunny," he shot back. "Freezing in Chicago still?"

"Not nice, is it really warm and sunny?"

He laughed once. "No. It's forty-seven degrees and going to rain."

"I actually feel better now, thanks. Is Hope with you?"

Zane smiled as he reached a stoplight. "Nope. Baby girl is at home in bed, sorry. You weren't calling me to talk to her, were you?"

"I'll never tell, but while I've got you . . ." She broke off for a quick laugh. "What are you doing in like ten days?"

"Probably playing hockey . . ." He thought out his schedule quickly, gently tapping the gas pedal as the light turned green. "That's right around Hope's birthday, and it might actually be a long stretch. Why? Whatcha got?"

He heard her rummaging around, saying something he didn't catch to someone there with her. "Sorry, Grizz needed my chair."

"What? Rude. You tell that guy I got his number if he's swiping your chair."

Bree erupted in laughter. "Right, okay, that's my new favorite image. Anyway. Think you can get up here for a dedication of the new team room?"

Zane frowned in thought. "Wait a sec, it's done? That was supposed to take another month at least."

"I know! But they pulled out a miracle, and they want to dedicate it ASAP. Get this—we're naming it after Coach Fenwick."

A smile flashed across Zane's face at that. "Perfect. I'm in, if I can. Lemme check a few things, and I'll text you tonight. That work?"

"Absolutely. Hey, Zane? Bring Hope with you. I missed her last time."

He nodded in secret delight that Bree wouldn't see, loving how the entire group had adopted his daughter. "I can do that. Gotta go, Bree. Talk to you soon." He hung up and shook his head, laughing at the sheer madness that had been this rejuvenation of Northbrook.

It was worth it in at least a dozen ways, and he would do far more than he had done, if required, to see the program saved. Reconnecting with his old teammates might be the best part. They'd never been super close when they were teammates, but in adulthood, they had formed a sort of brotherhood that meant a lot to him these days.

Funny how that worked.

Zane shook himself as he pulled into the parking lot of the community center, grinning as he practically jumped out of the car and headed in. He couldn't say that he had been here before, unless it had been to check out the daycare for Hope, but it couldn't be too difficult to navigate.

Once he entered the building, it was actually pretty straightforward. He followed the sounds of tennis shoes squeaking loudly, of a ball hitting the floor with incredible force, and of the unmistakable mixture of laughter, groans, and cheers that spoke of friendly competition.

It made him smirk to think of that. There was nothing friendly about his kind of competition.

The first gym had an actual team, so he moved to the second, and he paused at the door, watching for a minute.

A ragtag group of people filled both sides of the court, varying in height but not ability. They went all out, and the guys showed no mercy on the girls. *Or the girls on the guys,* he thought as a girl who had to be six foot three slammed a spike down with such force, the guy playing back row in the path of the ball dove *away* from it.

That was Zane's kind of game, and he had no shame in admitting it.

The girl whooped and turned, punching a fist in the air and slapping hands with her teammates.

A brunette with killer legs and a perfectly fitted workout tank gave her double high fives, then slipped an arm around her back as they walked over to get water, the set apparently over now. There was no mistaking Mara among this crowd, and her smile was infectious. Then she laughed, tossing her head back, the sound carrying in the open gym.

Zane's chest tightened at the sight of her, the sound of her, but his lips curved in helpless delight.

She looked towards the door as she reached for her water and froze, her eyes going wide.

He entered the gym, eyes on her, and smiled as though she weren't stunned to see him. "Hi."

Slowly, Mara straightened. "Zane? What are you doing here?"

"I thought I'd come and play some volleyball," he offered as he neared her. "You said this is what you do for fun, and I wanted to have fun with you. Is that okay?"

Her mouth worked on an answer she couldn't seem to form, though the others in the room were suddenly very interested in what was going on between them. "You shouldn't be here."

Yeesh . . . He grimaced a little. "Too much? Sorry, I can go if you'd rather . . ."

"No!" she said quickly, stepping towards him. "No, not like that. It's just that . . ." She came closer, dropping her voice. "You shouldn't be playing volleyball right now. You're in season, you could hurt yourself."

Zane gave her a crooked smile, the tightness in his chest easing significantly now that he was close to her, and now that she didn't object to his coming. "Why don't you let me worry about hurting myself?"

She frowned at him. "You have a game tomorrow! What are you going to tell your coaches if you sprain an ankle?"

"If you think a fun game of volleyball is going to hurt me enough to keep me from the ice," he told her firmly, "you've got another thing coming." He quirked a brow, then took his phone and keys from his pocket, setting it down by her stuff. "You gonna introduce me, or should I do the honors?"

Mara started to smile, shaking her head. "You're crazy."

"Not the first one to notice, babe." He winked and turned to the others. "Hey, y'all. My name's Zane, and I call permanent spot on whatever team Mara's on."

Every girl in the room oohed suggestively at his claim while the guys nodded in appreciation, which said everything that needed to be said about men and women.

A choking sound behind him made Zane look over his shoulder.

Mara's cheeks were flushed, but her smile was in place as she stared back at him.

"What?" he asked unapologetically.

"You're the sweetest crazy person I know," she replied, the curve of her smile warming him from the inside out. "Even when you embarrass me."

He tossed a playful grin at her. "Nothing embarrassing about staking my claim. Come on, let's show this crowd what we've got."

Mara tilted her head, one hand propping on her perfectly trim hip. "You don't know how I play."

There were several answers he could have given, but he settled for holding a hand out to her. "So show me what you've got, Matthews. I'm a fan of those legs already, but I'm willing to like them more."

"Very generous," she retorted as she took his hand and let him pull her onto the court.

"Yes, they are," he murmured softly, his mouth close to her ear as they moved into place.

She whirled and held a finger out at him, her color still high, laughing almost breathlessly. "Huh-uh. None of that, mister. We mean business on this court."

"What?" He gestured helplessly, looking around. "I can flirt and play seriously at the same time. It's called multitasking, right?" He turned to the woman playing back row behind him. "Am I right?"

The woman shrugged and grinned wickedly at Mara. "I think so. Go for it. Anything to keep Mara on her toes is fair game."

"Traitor." Mara made a face at her, then turned back to the net, raising her hands in position. She glanced over at Zane, smiling again. "Hey."

He matched her pose and smiled back. "Hey what?"

She bit her lip slightly, and his knees almost buckled. "I missed you."

It was a good thing the other team served the ball at that moment, or he would have marched over to that woman and carried her from the court to kiss her senseless. Fortunately for everyone in the room, his competitive side kicked into gear, and he was only lightheaded for the first three points.

That the other team scored.

Not okay.

"That was low," Zane muttered as he watched the server through the net.

Mara laughed from his left. "What was?"

"You can't say something like that to a guy when he can't reciprocate," he informed her, watching as the ball soared over them to their back row. "It's rude."

"It's strategic," Mara corrected him as she set the ball beautifully to the guy on the far left of their court.

Zane grunted as the other team returned the hit, now setting up their attack. "How's that?"

All business, she followed the play opposite them, coming right to his side. "Well . . ." She paused as they jumped as one to block the ball, the defensive specialist digging it nicely. "You're good at making me flustered. Time for payback."

"Oh." They turned slightly as the ball came back over the net, their back row sending it up to them. "Just one problem."

Mara set him the ball, again beautifully. "Yeah?"

He nodded as he jumped, spiking the ball hard to the opposite side of the net, without any answer. Their team cheered and slapped hands, which he took, but he looked at Mara only. "I'm competitive. You just cranked up the game."

Her eyes widened, and her smile turned a little shaky, but she was laughing through it. "Uh-oh."

"Game on, Matthews," he replied, turning back to face the net, smiling at no one in particular as their team served for the first time that match.

Driven by more than just their team's score, Zane and Mara both played with more energy, and Zane, for one, was elated to discover that Mara's competitive drive rivaled his own. She was completely in every play, sacrificing her body as she dove for balls and not backing down from any chance she could get to block or spike. She wasn't the tallest woman on the court, and certainly most of the guys were taller than her, but she was a fierce player. And she had the most wicked serve he had ever seen, and it took the other team at least five serves to figure out how to answer it.

It did need to be stated that Mara was way more sportsmanlike than Zane, though, which was probably the biggest difference in all this.

But when he was playing beside her, he was way more sportsmanlike too.

Didn't stop him from excessive celebration when his team made a kill or when someone made a particularly spectacular play, but he wasn't yelling at anyone either.

Little things.

His team didn't seem to mind his enthusiasm, though. On the contrary; they were right along with him, high fives, chest bumps, picking each other up, and all.

Well, maybe he was the only one picking anyone up, and maybe it was just Mara, but no one seemed to mind.

Least of all Mara.

They'd won the first match and were now hard into the second, hovering at match point as they had been for at least three serves. The other team had come back in a big way already, the momentum squarely in their favor. His team had managed to get the last point, the ball now on their side, and

Zane wasn't about to let this go to a third match that may never be settled, in his mind. One glance at the clock on the wall told him that they didn't have enough time to finish a third, even if they started it, and who knew when he'd be able to get back over here on a Monday to finish it out?

"Here we go, Brady," he chanted, clapping his hands, keeping his attention forward as Brady prepared to serve behind him.

Zane heard Mara exhale slowly beside him, and he felt his lungs release air in response. He glanced over to see her bent over, jaw set, swaying slightly on her poised feet, eyes on the players opposite them. She was ready.

And she was gorgeous. Powerful and captivating, the sort of woman he'd always admired and yet had never fallen for.

His brows shot up as the thought flashed in his mind, and he returned his attention to the game.

Fallen? That was going a bit far, considering they weren't even dating. Not really. They were just ... they were ...

What? What were they, and what were they doing?

Brady served the ball then, and Zane shook away the distracting thoughts of Mara. Clean dig, going up for a set, and then ...

"TIP!" he shouted to his team.

But Mara was there, already dropped to her knees to set the ball up and away from the floor.

"Here!" Kath called from behind her, setting beautifully over to Zane.

He was already in the air before it got to him, and he swung back, connecting with the ball in perfect time, sending it screaming to the court, right between two defenders.

"RAH!" he bellowed in victory, clenching his fists and turning to his team. "Yeah!"

Mara whooped loudly, holding her splayed hands out,

her face wreathed in elation. She slapped hands with Kath hard, then turned to Zane, stunning him by jumping into his arms. He caught her easily, his arms going around her midriff and spinning her around once as they cheered.

"Yeah, baby!" Mara exclaimed as she clung to him. "Woo!"

Their team swarmed them, jumping up and down, slapping hands and backs, their praises almost unintelligible in the melee. Somehow, Mara was pried from his hold, though one of his arms managed to stay clamped around her waist.

He'd like to see someone try to get her away from him completely right now.

"That dig, Mars!" Brady was saying, giving her a high five. "Killer."

"Did you see flying monkey man over here?" Kath retorted, jerking a thumb at Zane. "I think the earth moved with that hit."

"More like a flying Zamboni," Mara said with a laugh.

The group froze and looked at her for a moment. Zane bit back a grin, waiting for the other shoe to drop.

"No . . . way . . ." one of the guys from the other side said, coming over to the net for a better look.

"Whoops," Mara muttered beside Zane. "Sorry . . ."

Zane squeezed her closer. "No worries. I don't mind."

"Zamboni?" another guy said, ducking under the net. "*The* Zamboni? Seriously?"

Zane gestured helplessly and grinned. "Guilty as charged. What's up?"

At least three guys came over and shook his hand, and the women looked him over with new appreciation.

"I had no idea, man," someone was saying. "Absolutely killer game. You're a beast."

"Thanks, you're not a bad player yourself."

"You're . . . you're coming back, right?" the first one said. "To play again?"

Zane shrugged but smiled easily. "In season is a bit rough, schedule-wise, so I don't know. Out of season, though . . ." He nodded slowly. "I own you, bro."

Brady barked a laugh and slapped Zane's hand over the heads of the group. "Man, I don't care what anyone says, I call forever teammate whenever you show up."

Zane grinned at him and nodded. "You got it."

"We can't *all* be with Zane every time," Mara chortled, giving her friend a sardonic look. "Come on."

"Some people can," he murmured for her alone, his arm around her waist tightening with his meaning.

Her throat worked at that, and he smiled at seeing it, smug satisfaction hitting him at how she stiffened beneath his hand. But she wasn't moving away. At all.

Game, set, match.

Patting her waist softly, Zane looked over at the other court. "We done, guys?"

One of the guys over there picked up a white towel and waved it in the air. "Uncle."

"Oh, please," Kath snorted. "Those were the best two sets we've had in a long time."

"Truth," Mara agreed with a nod, shifting her weight to actually lean further into Zane, folding her arms.

Now he was the one swallowing.

"Ice cream?" Mara asked of the group. "Anyone?"

There were quite a few headshakes and denials, and a jolt of excitement shot down Zane's left leg.

"I'm in," he murmured.

Mara looked up at him, her lips curving to one side. "Why does that not surprise me?"

He shrugged and walked with her to their stuff, sliding

his hand away from her waist but keeping contact as long as he could.

He heard her clear her throat as she picked up her bottle of water and purse. "Okay, y'all, see you next week!"

They called out their farewells, and Mara turned to Zane. "Ready?" he asked.

She nodded. "You?"

"One thing." He tossed his arm around her shoulder and held his phone up, camera on. "Smile!"

She did so, holding two thumbs up, then laughing at the photo. "What are you going to do with that?"

He dropped his arm and pressed a few buttons on his phone, shooting the pic off to the Pit. "Nothing. Some people need to see this."

"Do they? Hmm." She shook her head and started walking for the door with him.

Sliding his phone into his pocket, he glanced at her. "So where do you get ice cream around here?"

"Usually Benny's." She shrugged and grinned up at him. "But if it's just us, it doesn't matter."

He returned her grin. "Not really, no." Holding his breath, he swung his hand out to take hers, then waited as they walked.

She laced her fingers with his automatically, and again came the sensation that his knees were no longer in place.

And there went the loopy grin again.

*Fallen,* his mind said again.

It was certainly something to consider at this point, though it seemed ridiculously fast.

But Mara wasn't Michelle. He'd known her for a number of days, but he'd known Michelle for years before they married and would never have suspected how that would go.

No telling where this would lead.

He only knew where he'd like it to lead, and at this moment, that was ice cream.

Or anywhere, so long as it was with Mara.

They stepped outside only to find rain pouring down. He swore softly and made a face, while Mara only laughed and started running for it.

"Where are you going?" he called, chasing after her.

"My car, duh," she yelled back. "I got front-row parking tonight!"

He followed, starting to laugh just as she was, the rain pounding down on them with more power than they usually saw in February. He continued to laugh until they finally reached her silver car.

"Anytime now would be great," he commented ruefully from the passenger door.

"Not helping," she hollered back.

Finally she had unlocked the door, both of them scrambling in out of the rain.

Zane laughed as he slammed his door shut. "That was a riot."

"The rain or the game?" Mara asked, shoving her purse behind her seat, breathless from their run.

"Both." He leaned his head back against the seat with a sigh. "You wouldn't believe how good it feels to get out and do something that isn't related to hockey or my daughter." He rolled his head on the headrest to look at her. "Don't get me wrong, Hope is my everything."

"I know," Mara told him quietly, her gentle smile putting him at ease. "I can see that."

He returned the smile, startled by how comfortable it felt to sit in a car with Mara and talk. "But this is just nice."

She nodded slowly. "It really is."

"How was your day?" he asked, settling into his seat as though it were an easy chair.

Mara snorted softly. "Typical. Patients were fine, and the office was a minefield."

That surprised him, and he watched Mara more closely. "How so?"

She leaned back against her seat, shaking her head and wetting her lips. "I work with the greatest doctor ever. Good with patients, amazing at his job, efficient enough to keep a good flow, never gets stressed out. He's incredible."

"What's the problem?" Zane asked, feeling lost.

"Our office lead," Mara all but spat. "Susan. She's not our boss, but she thinks she is. Threatens to write us up if we don't do what she wants. Sends passive-aggressive emails to the whole office instead of coming directly to anyone. Has favorites in the department." A bitter smile crossed Mara's perfect lips. "She doesn't like my doctor. Or me."

A sudden burst of fury lit up Zane's chest, and he all but growled, "Why?"

Mara looked at him, brow raised. "We don't do things her way. Simple as that. She'd get rid of both of us, our entire team, and at least six others. Likes to pit people against anyone not on her good list."

"How did Susan get in a position of any authority?" Zane demanded in disgust.

"She knows everyone." Mara shrugged, seeming almost defeated now, which Zane hated immediately. "No one believes our complaints."

Zane shook his head in disbelief. "Why do you stay, Mara?"

"My doctor. And waiting for an opening in the ER to transfer." Then she smiled almost sheepishly. "And I don't want to give Susan the satisfaction of getting rid of me."

"Atta girl!" Zane laughed. "This is why I play hockey. I can hit people who make my life crap."

Mara's smile grew mischievous. "So if I had an office social on the ice..."

He nodded once. "Susan would be toast."

"Love it. Can we reserve the rink now, or...?"

Zane chuckled and reached out to take Mara's hand again, not hesitating to link her fingers with his now.

Her thumb brushed against his skin softly. "I can't imagine anyone making your life crap, Zane."

He laughed once. "You need to work on your imagination, then. It's a full-time occupation for some."

"But... they know you'll hit them in the game."

"Yep."

"Why not just ignore them?"

"Shutting them up is way more fun. And effective."

Mara snickered, then sighed, the sound automatically tightening his grip on her hand. She looked down, one of her fingers absently tracing a pattern on her leg. "Can I ask you something?"

The hesitant question made him curious. "Sure."

"Why don't you like Valentine's Day?"

Was that all? He smiled at her, though she wasn't looking. "A lot of fuss, I've always thought. And Michelle always expected grand gestures, also known as expensive gestures, and I constantly failed. She complained I wasn't proving my love for her when it mattered most."

"That's not fair."

"That's what I thought too. Doesn't love matter most when it's not forced? The everyday stuff should have proof in it. Not one day just because everyone else is." He shrugged a shoulder, brushing his fingers against hers. "I'd rather have a night at home in my sweats and eating a pizza, honestly."

Mara hummed softly. "Low-key. Comfortable. No stress. Sounds perfect."

Zane smiled at her. "Why'd you ask?"

"Just curious. Hope seemed pretty certain you don't like it."

"Does that bother you?" he pressed in as gentle a tone as he could manage, holding his breath. "As I recall, you said you loved it."

Mara met his eyes with a wide grin. "For the chocolate. It's the best time of year for that."

Zane laughed, turning more fully towards her. "That's it?"

She tilted her head playfully. "Technically the day after Valentine's Day is my favorite. Chocolate is on sale. I celebrate every year."

Unreal. She was the most interesting, natural, genuine woman he had ever met in his entire life. And he wanted more.

"Sounds perfect," he murmured. "Shall we go get ice cream?"

Mara flicked a smile in his direction. "Honestly, I'm good right here."

"So am I."

# TEN

MARA HAD NEVER had Valentine's Day plans in her entire life.

Ever.

There wasn't really a reason for it, unless one counted the fact that she had never been in a serious relationship worth celebrating on Valentine's Day.

Today that would change.

Not that she was in a relationship, technically. She wasn't. Officially.

But she'd never wanted anything more in her entire life. She wanted Zane Winchester, and she wanted him bad.

Which was why she was doing something that could potentially blow up in her face, although she suspected it would actually win her some serious points with him.

She hoped it would.

Ever since her long talk in the car with Zane on Monday night, she'd been cooking this up. They'd talked for hours, and she'd felt the late night the next morning at work, but the day had been too busy in the clinic for her to care that much. That, and she'd been giddy most of the time.

That was probably also in part due to sleep deprivation, but she was definitely into Zane as well.

And somehow, in some way, he was into her too.

She hadn't quite figured that one out yet, but she'd take full advantage of it.

If all went well tonight, she'd have a solid tally in her favor.

He'd had a fantastic game in New York the night before, and they'd been texting each other all day, so she had a fairly good idea of where his head was at. Not that it mattered to her nerves, which were on high alert. That whole fight-or-flight response was definitely skewed to the flight part, and the only reason she wasn't fleeing into the night was that her hormones were in charge at the moment.

And they wanted her to floor it.

She pulled into his neighborhood, clamping down on her lip hard, her heart tap-dancing in her throat.

This was her staking her claim.

He'd said he was doing that the other night, and now it was her turn. If he didn't see this gesture for what it was, she'd have some serious waking up to help him with.

Potentially by smacking him on the shoulder using any valentines his daughter had left over from her school party.

Just for symbolism.

Mara exhaled slowly as she pulled into the driveway, her eyes darting across every window just to see which lights were on. She hadn't gotten the tour of upstairs when she'd been by before, but the lack of light there at least had her convinced Hope would be asleep.

Which was what she'd wanted.

A window showed lights on the main floor, and a moment of panic struck her as she considered that Josie could be staying over that night. Zane was in town, so it wasn't likely, but she hadn't checked on his schedule for tomorrow. If he had an early practice . . .

She shook her head, fighting back the rising anxiety. One step at a time. She could adapt to the situation as needed, and everything would still work out.

So long as she didn't have to drop off the pizza and leave.

She had specifically planned the outfit she wore and redone her hair three times just to make sure everything worked.

Turning the key in the ignition, she exhaled a sputtering breath, eyeing the front door. It was now or never, and never just wasn't an option.

Mara climbed out of the car and grabbed her purse, closed her door, then walked around to the passenger side of her car and got her reinforcements. Kicking the door shut, she started up the stone path to the front door, pausing only for a moment when the motion-sensor lights kicked on and startled her. She shook her head as she forced herself to keep going, stepping up on the porch and knocking on the front door before sliding back a step.

One of her legs bounced with barely contained energy as she waited, ears straining for the sound of footsteps within the house. Her pulse jumped when she heard it, and then she could make out, through the frosted glass of the door, the shape of an exceptionally well-built man she happened to admire very much.

She forced a smile on her face as the door pulled open, and she found the smile easier to maintain once the sight of Zane was before her.

Particularly when he wore such a beautiful look of surprise.

"Mara?" He looked her up and down, smiling as he did so. "What are you doing?"

She lifted her left leg a little off the ground. "Sweats." Then she gestured to the rest of her. "Casual." Hefting the pizza box in her right hand up a little, she quirked her brows. "Pizza."

Zane's eyes darkened, his smile turning hot. "I see."

She shrugged and quirked her brows. "Sounds like it's Valentine's Day or something. Feel like not celebrating with me?"

"Hell yeah." He stepped back, gesturing her in. "Get in here."

Knees shaking with relief and overwhelming hormonal impulses, she did so, handing over the pizza and slipping out of her shoes. "I was going to wear slippers, but it's still kinda raining, and I don't have the nice ones with the good tread on them."

"I think I'll survive the deprivation of your slippers." He looked down at the pizza, then shook his head and looked at her again. "I can't believe you did this."

Forcing herself to be controlled, Mara only made a face. "Don't make something out of the anti-Valentine's activity. No grand gestures here. That's the rule."

"That's true," he murmured, though his tone sent shivers up her arms and legs. His eyes dropped to her left hand. "What's in the bag?"

She slung the plastic bag over her shoulder. "Ice cream."

"Nice!"

"For me," she clarified firmly. "Rules are rules. You're on your own." Turning on the spot, she all but marched herself into the kitchen to get a spoon for herself, her heart pounding so hard she could feel it in her ears.

Had she really pulled that off? She had planned everything down to the words she'd say, had scripted at least seven alternatives, and at this moment, she felt like she'd just nailed a freaking highlight reel of possibilities. She exhaled slowly as she reached the kitchen island, opening a drawer to find silverware on the first try. Even more perfect.

Now all she needed was . . .

A pair of strong arms wrapped around her waist, pulling her back against a wall of muscle. Her body melted against Zane as he tucked her shoulder under his chin, just holding her close to him, neither of them moving further.

Heat spread from her toes on up, and she closed her eyes, letting herself feel every inch of him where they touched. His mouth suddenly pressed into her shoulder, more as a nuzzle than a kiss, but it electrified her all the same.

"Hey," he murmured into the fabric of her T-shirt, the movement of his lips tickling the painfully sensitive skin beneath what was suddenly a feebly thin layer.

Mara swallowed a lump of restrained desire before replying, "Hey."

"Do you have any idea," he told her softly, his mouth shifting up just enough to be clear of her shirt, "how amazing you are?"

Mercy . . . Her legs began to quiver, and she prayed he wouldn't notice.

"Or how incredible you look in sweats?" he went on, his voice dipping just enough to make her bite her lip.

Forget highlight reel. This was above and beyond imagination, and she was going to wake up tangled in her sheets panting and sweating in a minute.

"Or," he went on, determined to torture her into combustion, "how good you smell when you smell like pizza?"

Her eyes sprang open at that, a laugh bubbling up.

Okay, so maybe she wouldn't combust.

She rubbed one hand over the arms holding her waist and leaned to her left just enough to look at him. "You're really trying hard for that ice cream, aren't you?"

His grin was blinding in its brilliance, though the same heat she'd felt from his words lingered in his eyes. "Did it work?"

"Hmm." She shook her head, reaching for the spoon she'd retrieved. She pried open the lid of her pint, dug in for a scoop, then fed it to him, patting his arms as she did so. "Here you go."

Zane groaned in apparent delight at the ice cream, winking at her. "Good stuff." His arms slid from her waist, and he patted her hip with a familiarity that almost took out Mara's knees again. "Wanna watch something while we eat?"

"Sure," she somehow managed without sounding breathless. "I was actually wondering . . ." She trailed off, wincing at the thought.

He paused while getting plates and turned to look at her. "You gonna finish that, or am I supposed to guess?"

She scowled, which only made him laugh. "Can we watch a hockey game?"

He turned, plates in hands, surprise evident. "Well, sure, but why?"

"I don't really know the game as well as I'd like to," she said, wrinkling her nose with her admission. "As I now have an increased appreciation for it . . ."

He took a bow. "Thank you, thank you."

"I thought," she went on, ignoring him, "why not have an expert help me understand more?"

"Fair point." He came to her and set the plates down, brushing a strand of hair off of her brow and leaving a scorching path against her skin. "I'd be happy to teach you. One condition."

Her eyes narrowed. "Okay . . ."

He gave her a slow smile. "You don't cheer for anyone but me."

Okay, that was insanely cute, if a little possessive. She could live with that.

"If I must," she replied, reaching out to toy with the hem of his T-shirt a little. "I have a condition myself."

"Shoot." His voice wobbled in its attempt to be carefree, and her confidence skyrocketed.

She grinned and rocked up on her tiptoes. "I get you as a pillow."

His exhale came in a gust, and his nod seemed a little rushed. "Gotcha. Can do."

"Good." She lowered herself and grabbed a plate, moving away from him to the pizza. "Who's playing tonight, and do we care how it goes?"

*We.* She hadn't meant to say it, hadn't thought she'd say it, hadn't meant anything by saying it, but now that it was said . . .

She liked that word.

She liked it a lot.

If Zane noticed, he gave no indication.

"Lucky for you, we have options." He reached over the island for three slices of pizza, then dropped them onto his plate before heading out to the great room, waving for her to join him. "You can decide if we watch a game we care about or if we watch a throwaway."

Mara sighed almost silently as she followed, heart swelling within her at how comfortable this was. How fun. How *real.* Just two people who liked each other flirting, hanging out, and enjoying being together. It was the most low-key thing in the world, but it felt like so much more. It felt serious without the weight of something serious.

What did that mean for them?

"Do you have anyone you're supposed to be paying attention to?" she asked, rounding the sectional and sitting next to him. "The next team you play or something?"

He shook his head as he picked up a remote and started scrolling. "Trust me, I watch plenty of film on upcoming teams, I don't need additional homework. Oh, here we go.

Comets against Hawks. These are pals of mine, so let's see who takes home the win. Then I can roast them with more accuracy."

"Because that's important."

He dropped an arm around her shoulders with a comfortable casualness she loved, and she leaned into him in an automatic response. "Well, yeah. You don't want to be wrong in a roast."

She nodded as she took a bite of pizza. "Of course not. Silly me."

The game on, Zane picked up his phone. "Okay, two seconds while I get this started . . ."

Mara looked at his phone with a smile. "They're on the ice, how can you roast them now?"

"Not them." He grinned at her quickly, then returned his attention to the screen. "The guys. There's like six of us from Northbrook that have reconnected, and we've got this group text . . . That's who I sent the pic from volleyball the other night to, by the way."

"Oh good," she remarked dryly. "I'm sure they had great things to say when I was all sweaty and nasty."

Zane gave her a scolding look. "Sweaty, maybe. Comes with a hard game. Nasty? Never." He winked and returned his attention to the phone. "And they thought you looked great. Wondered how I got within five feet of you."

Mara scoffed around a bite of pizza. "Uh-huh. Sure they did."

"See for yourself." He held the phone out to her, text pulled up.

She took it from him and scrolled, smiling even as her eyes widened.

*Trane: Dude . . .*

*Clint: Who let you on a VB court?*

*Jax: How much did you pay her to smile?*

*Rocco: Five feet. You got an attractive woman to let you within five feet. How does it feel?*

*Declan: Please tell me she owned you*

*Trane: But seriously, Z. Where did you find her?*

Mara grinned outright at Zane's response to them all.

*Zane: Finders keepers. If you're lucky, you'll meet her. Maybe.*

Various responses came up from that, but she pushed the phone back to him. "Great group."

"They're all right." Zane slid his phone to the table with a shrug. "Hope calls them her uncles, even though she's only known them four months."

"She's so cute," Mara told him, shaking her head. "Seriously."

Zane chuckled as he took a bite of pizza. "She knows it, too. Trust me."

"So what did you say to the group?" she asked as she propped her feet up on the coffee table, crossing her ankles. "About these guys?"

"Heh." Zane shook his head, drumming his fingers on her shoulder. "Just placing bets. Fido's on a roll, and Diesel is a fortress, so it's gonna be a great game."

Mara glanced at him, waiting a beat. "I have no idea what that means," she admitted without shame.

"Don't worry," he replied, tugging her closer. "I got you."

The next few minutes were spent pointing at the huge screen and indicating various positions, pointing out plays and illustrating penalties. Mara would admit to being intrigued by what she was learning, though she was equally distracted by snuggling up against a gorgeous, warm, incredibly virile man. If she remembered anything from the night, it would more than likely be the exact planes of the man she was curled against and how intoxicating he smelled, rather than any hockey terms or positions.

She wouldn't mind that so much.

Zane seemed to appreciate her putting forth the effort, and before long, the two of them were cheering every time Fido got the puck and cheering equally as hard when Diesel stopped any shot on goal. It was strange, cheering for players and not a team, especially when the players in question were on opposite teams, but Mara found it was actually a pretty enjoyable way to spend a game.

Eventually, though, she found herself getting sleepy, and Zane as a pillow was beyond comfortable. He never once complained about her snuggling closer, laying her head against him, or grabbing a blanket and pretty much actually turning him into her personal pillow. There was something incredibly soothing about the way he ran the edges of a few fingers up her spine, swirling them around her shoulder blade and down her arm.

"I'm going to close my eyes for a second, okay?" she murmured, her words as fuzzy as her head as she hugged herself flush against his side. "You're just really comfy."

"I aim to please," came the rumbling reply she felt as much as she heard. His fingers trailed up her back again, pausing to fiddle with her loosening hair before tracing back down again.

Mara nearly moaned in satisfaction, but she sighed instead, the sound quickly fading as she drifted off.

A few moments later, she yawned and stretched, then paused, frowning. How could she stretch her entire body out when she was basically lying on Zane? Licking her parched lips, moisture returning to her mouth, she pried her eyes open, staring up at the ceiling.

Right ... Lying down, not lying on Zane. Definitely not

in her room, so still at Zane's house. Little bit of light from the wall of windows behind her. Not nighttime. And if the feeling in her mouth was any indication, she'd been sleeping for a lot longer than a few moments, and with her mouth wide open.

That would have been really attractive.

Oh good.

Blinking, Mara exhaled slowly, shaking her head against a pillow beneath her head. She'd fallen asleep, and fallen asleep hard, during the end of the hockey game. For whatever reason, Zane hadn't seen fit to wake her up, which was going to throw off her entire morning routine . . .

Her eyes widened, and she sat up with a panicked gasp, looking around frantically for a clock of any kind. Morning-routine kinks were not good; she had timed everything out perfectly and was able to prepare for her day flawlessly on schedule, day in and day out. She was fifteen minutes from her place, had no scrubs in her car, and would either need a shower or some serious dry shampoo to be remotely presentable for work.

Not good. At all.

She jumped up from the couch and whirled around, wondering where in the world Zane kept a stupid clock when she caught sight of one.

6:43.

Oh crap.

"Gah!" she exclaimed, running into the kitchen and turning on the faucet, splashing some of the cold water onto her face. "Why why why why *why*?"

"Gonna need a little more than 'why' to answer the question," a teasing voice came from the stairs.

Mara spun on the spot, glaring in Zane's general direction even as water dripped from her face. "Why didn't you wake me last night? Zane, I have to work!"

"I know," he said simply as he continued to calmly pull his damp hair back into the small bun she was getting so used to. "I went on a run this morning and got you some coffee." He pointed to the counter, but Mara didn't look.

"Why?" she said again, grabbing a hand towel and dabbing her face.

He leaned against the stair railing with a maddening smile. "Because you were out last night and I didn't want you driving home that tired. Because I didn't feel like moving you off of me until I absolutely had to. Because you're beautiful even in your sleep and tucking you in on my couch was surprisingly moving and incredibly hot." He shrugged a shoulder. "Take your pick. All are true."

Mara blinked at him, swaying where she stood just for a moment, letting that sink in. Then she shook herself, her brow snapping down. "Well, you've just made my morning insane." She moved to the fridge and yanked it open, hoping he'd stuck the pizza in there. Sure enough, a box sat on the middle shelf, and she pulled it out just enough to open the lid and grab a slice. "Now I'm having cold pizza and coffee on the go for breakfast . . ."

"Okay . . ."

She balanced the precariously dangling slice in one hand as she closed the fridge, turning to swipe one of the coffees from the drink holder before she ran for the front door. "I have pretty much no time at home, which means either the fastest shower known to man or no shower at all. Do you know how hard it is to feel put together at the office without a shower? Impossible, that's how hard."

"My neighbor's a cop, I can get you an escort home so you can speed," Zane offered as he followed her, somehow still completely unflapped by her chaos.

"Ha!" She glowered at him as she balanced on one foot to

slip her tennis shoes on without untying them. "Funny. Because that's what I need, sirens and attention right now. Ugh!" She stumbled a little but got her balance before anything spilled. "Stupid shoes..."

She thought she heard Zane laugh, and she would have killed him if she'd had the time. "Can I help?"

"No," she ground out, shoving her toes into the other shoe and digging her heel in hard. "I think you have done quite enough, Hot Stuff, and unless you can get to my place before me so you can toss scrubs on me as I drive by..." She shook her head, grunting with satisfaction as she finally got the second shoe on. "Finally. Okay, bye."

She turned and wrenched the door open.

"Hey, Mara?"

"What?" she practically bellowed, whirling around, pizza in one hand, coffee in the other. "What, Zane?"

He was walking slowly towards her, a soft, crooked smile on his face. "You forgot something."

"Oh really?" she shot back, though his slinking towards her was setting her toes on fire. "Imagine that. What did I forget?"

His smile quirked wider for a second before he took her face in his hands and tilted it ever so slightly as his lips touched hers. Slowly, tenderly, his mouth moved against hers, his thumbs stroking a fiery pattern against her cheeks while he wrung every ounce of sanity and thought from her. Again and again, he took her lips, never pressing for more but leaving no doubt in her mind that he was in this. He wanted this.

He wanted *her.*

Her legs shook, and just as she opened for more, he pulled back, her lower lip catching in his with a faint tug that made something explode behind her belly button.

Zane's eyes searched hers, his breathing not quite steady,

but calmer than hers. His thumbs stroked her cheeks again. "Thanks for coming over last night," he whispered, his eyes dark and intense. "I loved it."

Mara stared back at him, trying to remember what words were and what lungs did, while her legs tingled from top to bottom. She swallowed, or tried to, and blinked, backing away, reminding herself not to drop the pizza or coffee. Or trip, slip, pass out, or stagger as she tried to make an escape that wouldn't be graceful or smooth even without incident.

"Okay," she said stupidly, her face flaming.

Zane shoved his hands into the pockets of his sweats, smiling at her, and gave her a little wave that made her heart flip. "Don't be late."

Late? Late for . . . ?

Oh. Late. Right.

Mara blinked again, then turned and dashed down the porch, down the drive, managing to slide into her car and have it on within a minute. Two seconds later, her seatbelt was on and she was backing out of the driveway, decidedly *not* looking anywhere near the porch, front door, or house.

Zane had kissed her. Zane had *kissed* her.

Zane had kissed the ever-loving crud out of her, and she wanted to scream at the top of her lungs, dance in the middle of the street, and lie on her bed and stare dreamily up at the ceiling while she relived every blistering moment of joy. She never wanted the tingling in her lips to fade, and she didn't particularly care if her legs ever stopped shaking.

But she was an adult and she had to work, and there was nothing she could do about that. She had to focus, keep it together, and be professional.

She bit down on her lip hard, letting a squeal release.

Okay, maybe not that professional, and maybe not that much of an adult.

But Zane had *kissed* her.

And she hadn't kissed him back. Not really, she'd just stood there and taken it.

Her eyes widened, and she gripped the steering wheel tightly. That kiss could have been better. Could be better. Could *get* better.

The soles of her feet suddenly began to heat as she considered that and as her imagination spun on the possibilities. Her stomach tensed, somehow linking into her lungs and forcing a harsh exhale from them.

This was going to build all day, and she would be an absolute mess by the end of it. Susan would be on her case when she was spacing out, but at this moment, Susan was the least of her concerns.

Zane Winchester was going to pay for upending her day and making her burn and burn and burn.

He was going to pay in a serious way, and she would collect at his game tonight.

Provided Mara made it through the day.

Her lips buzzed again in anticipation.

# ELEVEN

"Hard! Hard! Hard!"

Zane thumped the side of the boards, whistling repeatedly to his teammates on the ice. They'd had their work cut out for them with the Flyers, and now they were solidly in the third period without either team making much headway in the game. They were equally matched as teams, despite key players that stood out in various ways, and every person on the ice was playing their heart out.

Things were getting tense out there, and cheap shots were being taken.

It said a lot that Zane wasn't one of them.

He'd had his turn in the penalty box this game, of course. He just wasn't taking cheap shots.

He much preferred making a statement.

"Heads up!" Zane bellowed as his friend Jax Emerson broke into the Hounds' push on goal and swept the puck away. "Sweep! Sweep! Sweep!"

Vinny and Prom dropped back on defense while the forwards chased Jax as he plowed towards their goal. Prom moved up to intercept Jax but was neatly sideswiped by a Flyers winger as Jax easily swooped around him.

Zane shook his head with a scowl. Jax was a killer player, and it was clear the squad was having trouble shutting him up. Pike was having the game of his life in goal, only letting one of the Flyers' attempts through, but they really needed to do a better job of keeping the puck from getting that far.

Vinny covered Pike nicely and managed to knock Jax off course with a solid hit as they scuffled for the puck. Some quick ricochets, then Kelso was able to sneak in and sweep the puck out of the danger zone.

"Boomer, Zamboni, up!" Coach Wink called.

Zane sprang over the wall in an instant, Boomer hard behind him as they moved out into the ice. They both hovered around center ice, waiting for the play to take a side. Kelso passed to Ramsey, who moved deep into the ice.

Too deep.

"Easy!" Boomer bellowed as he drifted ahead. "Whoa! Whoa!"

But Ramsey was slammed into the boards by the Flyers' defense, the puck getting wrapped around the boards and coming up perfectly for Jax.

"Me," Zane grunted, though only Boomer would hear him. "Mine, mine."

He might have imagined it, but he thought Boomer chuckled.

Zane grinned slowly as Jax headed in his direction, starting to track his movements with some of his own. Jax was a tricky player, but years of practicing with him and against him at Northbrook, no matter how long ago, had left a muscle memory of sorts. Some habits were too hard to break, and if Zane's instincts were correct . . .

He laughed once as the puck came back to Jax, who still didn't seem entirely aware that Zane was out there.

Perfect.

Zane moved, weaving just enough to avoid targeting, then drove hard right at Jax.

Jax saw him, but too late, his eyes widening. "Oh sh—"

They collided hard into the boards, and Zane grunted as Jax's late attempt at a block caught him square in the chest. That earned his friend a second charge into the plexiglass, this time with more force.

"Hi, honey," Zane grunted, shoving off and heading for the goal, where Petey and Boomer tag-teamed the Flyer center, who'd managed to get the puck off Jax before impact.

He heard Jax roar behind him in a fired-up indignation, and he knew he wouldn't get a second hard hit on him without payback. Jax was a solid guy, terrific player, but he was also a hothead when it served him.

It would serve him tonight.

Zane tapped the ice quickly and saw the puck cross over to him, almost like he'd called it. He scooped, swung away, and bit back a curse himself as Jax now charged at him. One glance at his teammates told him he couldn't get it away easily on this side, and he immediately changed tactics.

And direction.

"Ollie! Ollie! Ollie!" he roared, cutting hard and racing back towards their own goal, the puck safely dribbling around his stick. He stuck close to the boards, eyes tracking incoming players, no matter who they played for, and he curved behind the goal, spitting quickly on the ice.

There was one problem with a retreat like this at a time like this.

Jax Emerson was one of the fastest guys on the ice.

And he was hot on Zane's tail.

"Mine!" Boomer announced, coming around for the rescue.

Zane flicked the puck to him just as Jax rammed him into the boards.

"Tag," Jax spat, practically bouncing off of him and keeping on the puck's path.

A dark growl erupted from the center of Zane's chest, and he bolted for Jax and Boomer, scuffling for the puck at the rear bar of the goal.

He jammed the toe of his stick between Jax's legs and tapped the puck out of their tussle, managing to sweep it away, but just barely.

The motion tripped Jax up, sending him to the ice on his back, while Zane dropped back to avoid being toppled himself. Seconds later, another Flyers wing charged at Zane in outrage, shoving him into the boards despite not having the puck anywhere near his possession.

Zane grabbed the guy's arm and launched him into the boards himself, more wanting to get the fool out of his way than start something.

But when a punch flew at his face, Zane snapped.

He whirled and grabbed the player's jersey, his fingers digging even into the pads for a better grip. He drove hard, trying to throw the guy down to the ice with as much force as one might use in a charge. His opponent was quick on his feet, though, and swung for him again, only slightly losing his balance.

Zane all but roared and rammed the player into the plexiglass, wishing he was near a bench so he could dump the pest into it.

A whistle blew, and Zane groaned at the sound, his temper still high, but his common sense belatedly kicked in.

"Nate!" Jax roared as he hunched over nearby, watching in disgust. "Cool it!"

Something about that name triggered Zane, and he glanced at his seething opponent. "Nate, huh?"

He received a dark look in return.

Zane smiled. "Cute. You defend your teammate even though you're nothing but a dirty hoser. You pay your coach to let you have five minutes on the ice, cupcake? Adorable. Maybe he'll even remember your name this time."

Nate snarled and charged at him again, but Zane ducked and backed away, hands raised.

The whistle blew again, and Nate almost got into a fight with the ref over the call.

It wasn't the classiest move on the ice, but Zane wasn't about to regret goading the kid into stupidity while the refs worked out the details of their fight. Natey-boy would get five minutes in the box, the Hounds would get a powerplay, and the Pit would light up their phones with various opinions on the subject. Dirty tactics, but it just might do the trick.

Zane exhaled slowly, shaking his head as he came around the goal again, surprisingly cool.

"Sweet moves, Z," Pike chuckled, taking a swig of water from the bottle on his net. "Nasty."

He nodded at the compliment but continued moving over to the faceoff area, eyeing any and all Flyers warily. They likely wouldn't appreciate being on the receiving end of that penalty, no matter how they felt about Nate in particular.

"Dude."

Zane snorted as he glanced over at Jax, hovering nearby. "Miss me?"

Jax glared, but Zane detected a smile beneath his friend's ever-impressive beard. "Not nice."

"Neither was his stunt with Meg." Zane shrugged and rested his elbows on his thighs while he waited.

"That was two months ago, Z. Trust me, we worked it out."

Zane smirked, looking at Jax again. "That was me working it out. I'm very sensitive to things like that."

Jax rolled his eyes, shaking his head. "She's my girlfriend, Z. I got it."

"I know you do. Doesn't mean I can't enforce it."

"He's still my teammate."

"He's still a punk."

"But . . ." Jax cut off suddenly.

Zane raised a brow. "But what?"

"Nah." Jax shook his head again. "You got me there. But I'd have pulled him off you if he got anywhere."

"I'd like to see you try." Zane groaned, craning his neck. "What is taking them so long?"

Jax scoffed softly, scooting closer. "Maybe they're scrambling to find a penalty for you."

"I was clean in that fight. Before the whistle, anyway."

"Uh-huh." The two of them shared a grin at that, knowing the truth.

The refs came over to faceoff now, and their attention returned to the game. "Loser buys dinner tonight," Zane grunted.

"Winner gets dessert," Jax shot back.

They clicked sticks on the bet, then charged forward as the puck dropped. Kelso scuffled with the Flyers' center, eventually getting the puck over to Ramsey, who raced out of their zone into central ice, moving play out of danger.

Zane swept right, crossing the center line while he eyed the play. The Flyers' front line swooped around, trying to cover for their teammate while he was on penalty, but the Kelso line was too quick and seemed to be continuously shooting on goal, though nothing was getting in.

A defender sent the puck up, trying to clear the ice, but Zane stopped it and swung it back into play, shoving Jax's teammate as he tried to take it.

Petey almost lost the puck but managed to save it by

driving into the boards and letting it drift back to Zane, who shot it over to center ice, where Kelso waited. He fired the puck at the goalie, but right at his pads for some reason. The puck ricocheted off, and Ramsey was there, slamming it into the goal just before the goalie could get all the way over.

The buzzer sounded, and the arena erupted with deafening cheers.

Zane whooped loudly and rushed in on Ramsey, tapping his helmet and shaking his pads with his excitement. Then Zane turned and gestured for the crowd to bring it up, to keep them energized, and they had no problem doing exactly that. Four minutes left in the third period, all they had to do was hold them off.

Easier said than done. The Flyers were well on their way to being number one in the league, and there was a reason for that.

The next faceoff proved just how difficult holding them off would be. Scuffling took longer than normal, players were getting punchy, and when the Kelso line pressed on goal again, Jax's line shifted out. Fresh legs were dangerous, and Zane made sure he and Boomer stayed on track, not that Boomer needed him to monitor. The guy was a hawk, and he barely celebrated anything on the ice until time ran out.

The Flyers made a move on goal, the Kelso line swapped out, but the new Flyers were hungry, and, try as Zane and Boomer did, they couldn't keep up. Even Pike was no match for their antics.

Zane swore under his breath as the buzzer sounded the goal. He came closer to Pike, who looked murderous.

"You good?" Zane grunted.

Pike glared at him. "Where were you?"

"Tap-dancing. Come on, that was a cheap shot in the corner pocket, and you know it."

"You gotta help me out, Z. Get there."

Zane nodded and skated back to his position.

Tied game.

If they could keep them tied until the end, they could get them in overtime. They were trained to skate longer and harder than any other team. That was the reputation of the Hounds these days, and they liked it that way

The Flyers were testing that claim, and it wasn't looking good.

Fortunately, Shap's line did not like their situation, and they made the Flyer goalie work to keep the tied game.

When the third period ended without a clear victory, rather than be upset about it, Zane felt a surge of excitement. They'd gone the distance with the hotshot team in the league, and no matter how this game ended, all of the other teams would know to watch out for the Hounds. A target on their backs, maybe, but so what?

Better to be targeted than to be written off.

Zane pumped up his teammates along with the captains as best as he could, though they didn't need much encouragement. They were all fired up all on their own, ready for overtime and to leave an impression.

The slate was clean now. New ice. New game.

Game on.

Coming back onto the ice was intense, and Zane loved it. The roaring of the crowd, the cool steel in the eyes of everyone, the possibilities before them . . .

This was the good stuff.

Flyers won the faceoff, the puck sliding towards Zane, Janny coming back to match him.

"Eyes, eyes, eyes," Zane chanted, backpedaling towards goal.

"Yeah," Janny replied, intercepting the play and sweeping it off to the side before charging up the ice.

Zane followed him, then groaned when the Flyers defender checked Janny, who then dropped his gloves and stick, challenging him. More gloves dropped, followed by a stick, and they were at it.

The Hounds box erupted, but Zane only watched, irritated. He was the showboat of the team, an enforcer and a penalty king, but this was just stupid.

Janny wasn't a fighter, and he would be owned by his opponent. This was pure temper tantrum, not the good hockey fights everyone could enjoy.

"You gonna defend your position?" Boomer asked, skating to his side.

"As what?" Zane replied. "Team Hothead? Even I don't fight pointlessly. I always have a reason."

Boomer barked a loud laugh. "Since when?"

"Now."

"Should we go break it up?" Boomer offered, making a face.

Zane shook his head. "If I set one foot over there, they'll call me on something. Shap can do it."

Sure enough, their team captain was to the fight in a moment, pulling the rookie off of the experienced defender almost twice his size. Shap yelled at Janny as he got pulled from the ice, and Zane grunted as they called the Flyers defender for the crosscheck.

"And on we go," Boomer acknowledged with a nod. "Your buddy should be shifting on soon. Got a present?"

Zane shrugged. "Maybe. Just want to get back to the good stuff. We're on fire, Boom. This should be fun."

"Should." Boomer gave him a look before moving to his side of the ice.

The play was back on, and sure enough, Jax was back on the ice within thirty seconds. He paid more attention to Zane, barely missing what would have been a glorious hit just as Boomer got slammed into the goal, dislodging the neck and stopping play.

Jax scooted backwards towards the faceoff, staring down Zane and shaking his head playfully.

Zane grinned and straightened, gesturing to himself as if to say *bring it on*, but he knew full well Jax wouldn't. It would take a lot for the two of them to actually fight each other, despite both being hotheads. Too much mutual respect and love of the game. They'd fight with other players, but not each other.

Hockey was strange that way.

The goal was righted—and another faceoff, this one moving quickly over to the goal. Zane chipped the puck out of danger, or so he thought, until Jax was back, scooping up the puck and firing it at the goal.

Zane blinked as the buzzer sounded, bringing the game to an abrupt end. The Flyers players swarmed Jax for his incredible play, and, for a moment, Zane felt as though his stomach dropped through the ice at his feet. But as he looked around the arena, the fans were still cheering their hearts out, undeterred by the loss and Jax's quick score.

They saw what Zane had seen.

The Hounds were on their way.

Zane nodded to himself and skated with his teammates over to the lineup, waving his stick in the air to the fans in thanks. They responded by pounding on the plexiglass and stomping their feet, which should ease the burden of his teammates.

Should.

They shook hands with the Flyers, and Zane patted Jax's face when they reached him. "Good shot, J."

"I like Italian," Jax told him, slapping his chest before moving on.

Zane rolled his eyes and finished the line before heading back to the locker room. He took a moment longer in the showers than he usually did, just because he would be taking Jax to dinner instead of going straight home.

The attitude of his teammates was lighter than it would normally be after a loss, and he was glad to see it. A loss to the Flyers after a game like that wasn't something to pout about. Sure, it could be a disappointment, but the attention on the sports programs wouldn't be about the Flyers dominating the Hounds. It would be about the street fight of a game and how the Flyers almost didn't pull it off.

That was a disappointment worth getting over.

Pulling a black T-shirt over his head, Zane reached for his phone, glancing at the screen before sliding it into his pocket with disgust.

Missed call from Michelle.

Again.

No voicemail.

This was getting ridiculous. His playing schedule was public knowledge; she could have figured out when he wasn't available. But effort wasn't something that interested his ex, and he shouldn't be surprised by that.

Jax would have a field day when he found out.

He grabbed his coat and bag, nodding to Flake and Petey as he headed out of the locker room. It would be fantastic to have a distraction from the drama that was guaranteed to be heading his way once he stopped missing her calls.

He didn't even want to consider what it could be.

He wasn't interested.

"Hey."

He hadn't expected the warm, familiar voice that made his pulse instantly dance, and he stopped, looking up, unsure when he had started looking down as he walked. His bag dropped to the ground once his eyes adjusted, and his pulse went from dancing to pounding in at least seven locations on his body.

Mara stood there, leaning against a cement pillar, her incredible legs encased in black leggings that disappeared into a long cream-colored tunic sweater with a wide neck. He could almost see the tops of her shoulders, though he could definitely see thin straps of a tank top beneath. She'd curled her hair a little, making it wave in a way that caused his fingers to itch with the desire to wrap themselves within it. Her makeup was only a little more than usual, he was pleased to see, with plenty of her all-natural beauty shining through. She'd worn neutral boots with a heel, and the gift that heel was to already perfect legs undid him.

"Hi," he exhaled, the word almost lost on the gust of air. "You . . . you were . . ."

She tilted her head a little, and his lips began to buzz, the memory of that morning's kiss reigniting with a fury. Somehow he'd forgotten all about that during his game, though he'd been turned around by it for most of the day. Her lips had been soft and generous, and if she hadn't backed away through his front door, he'd have gone in for another kiss far less simple.

Her left leg began to bounce a little, and his attention shifted there, blood pounding hard in his ears.

The leg moved, and he blinked, barely having time to register that Mara was coming towards him before she had one hand behind his head and had tugged his mouth to hers.

What followed was a thorough dismantling of every single thought Zane had ever had in his entire life.

There was zero hesitation in her kiss, and her hold on him bordered on the painfully clenching, which lit into him like an electric shock. One hand clamped against her hair, taking no care for whatever she'd done with it, while his other arm wrapped around her and hauled her closer. He fought with her passion, warred with it, danced with it, and took the kiss as deep as she would allow, though she was keeping him plenty occupied with the intoxicating give-and-take her lips were engaged in.

Zane moaned as she dug her fingers in against his neck and moved, pushing her back until there was a wall to support them both. Mara latched both hands onto his neck now, one beginning a slow slide up against his scalp that created an echo of rippling sensation up his spine. He gasped against her mouth, then slid his lips from hers to shower her jaw and neck with heat. Her gasps and whimpers into his ear spurred him on, but nothing undid him more than the powerful jerk he felt from her hands dragging his mouth back to hers.

Her lips were relentless against his, leaving no doubt in his mind that she was in control here, and she wanted *him*.

It was a humbling and gratifying sensation, and he softened his hold on her just enough to turn the kiss tender. No less powerful, no less intense, and she responded immediately, opening to him further still, now wrapping her arms around his neck in an embrace, sighing into him.

Zane's fingers tangled further into her hair, cradling this incredible woman against his mouth.

"Oh, come on, he didn't play *that* good."

They both froze at the jab, and a slow, burning trickle of indignation began in Zane's heels and moved up his calves. His lips still touched Mara's, though neither moved.

"Hmm," Jax said again, sounding completely unperturbed by what he was seeing. "So I'm guessing that's a raincheck for dinner . . ."

Zane brushed his lips very softly and very carefully against Mara's, a promise of continuation as soon as possible, before pulling back just enough to disconnect from her. He dropped one hand from the wall, though he wasn't sure when it had pressed there, and reached for his wallet in a back pocket. He held it out behind him, keeping his eyes trained on Mara's wide, almost slumberous ones. "Take the money."

Jax *tsked*, not taking the wallet. "Solo dinners. Not my fave. How about breakfast tomorrow? Bring the bug?"

Zane exhaled a short grunt, watching with almost pain as Mara's full and swollen lips quirked at the reference she clearly caught. "She has school, J."

"Tomorrow's Friday," Jax reminded him. "Late arrival. She told me last time we talked school."

Now Zane growled, earning him would-be soothing strokes from Mara's fingers against his neck. "J. I will end your season if you don't leave now."

"I'll text you the location for tomorrow," came the cheeky reply. "I'm serious, bring the bug. And whoever is between you and the wall."

Mara lifted a brow, smiling fully now, but only at Zane. "Mara."

"Hi, Mara. I'm Jax."

Zane leaned closer to Mara, her eyes darkening as he brushed his nose against hers. "The corpse formerly known as Jax in three . . . two . . . one . . ."

"Good night, guys. Drive safe. Oh, Z . . ."

"Jax . . ."

"See you next week?"

"Yes," Zane grunted. "Bye."

He didn't hear another response, so he took the opportunity to press his lips to Mara's again, though the damage was done and their whirlwind moment of passion was fading.

Or the delirium of it was.

He could happily kiss Mara in this long, lingering, slow way for ages without interruption.

Mara finally broke off, sighing deeply and running her fingers along his scalp again, reaching into his longer hair in a way that sent fire shooting into his gut. "That has been building all. Freaking. Day."

Zane grinned and nuzzled against her lips, catching her lower one with his teeth very softly. "Remind me to give you a kiss every morning, then."

"That was supposed to be payback," Mara scolded, her eyes narrowing.

"Yeah, I got that. Good job."

"Ha," she said softly, draping her arms over his shoulders and touching her brow to his. "So. Is Jax always like that?"

Zane shook his head against her, his thumb stroking against her cheek. "No. This is a special occasion."

Mara's giggle made him tense. "What's he like normally?"

"Not your type."

She gave him a scolding look. "That wasn't where I was going."

"Doesn't matter. 'Nuff said."

Mara sighed a laugh and laced her hands around him, leaning back against the wall. "Are you upset about the loss?"

He gave her a crooked smile "What loss? I haven't lost a damn thing tonight."

"Cute," she remarked, her cheeks coloring.

"No, incredible," he assured her. "I think my brain is moving backwards right now, and I'm wondering when we can do that again." He leaned in to give her another soft kiss. "I'm on fire, babe. For you."

Mara shivered in his hold, and he pulled her closer out of instinct. "Me too," she admitted in a whisper. "You should have seen me at work, I was a complete wreck."

"I'm not apologizing for that," he said, grinning freely. "I intend to be the foremost thought in your mind from here on out."

"You won't have to work very hard there." She lowered one of her hands to trace along the scruff at his jaw, her eyes following. "What do we do now?"

He heard the uncertainty in her voice, and it weakened his knees. He tipped her chin up, her eyes finding his once more. "You're driving this boat, babe. I'm just enjoying the ride."

Her eyes searched his with more raw vulnerability than he'd have ever expected in her. "So if I were to tell you to stop . . ."

"Hard stop," he interrupted firmly. "No arguments. I might cry a little, go beat something up, but no argument."

"What if I said . . . ?"

"Your pace," he insisted. "Whenever you're ready for wherever we go, I'm there."

"Even if I said snail?" she ventured.

He swallowed and nodded, still smiling. "Slow and steady works." He waited a beat, then winced. "You're not going to say snail, are you?"

Mara laughed and touched her nose to his. "No, dummy, I was just checking."

He exhaled roughly in relief. "Oh sweet mercy, thank you." He kissed her quickly, then pulled her in for a tight hug. "This is real, Mara. Really real. And while I am a huge fan of what just happened, I am even more a huge fan of *you*. I'm in this, okay? This is a thing. If you want it to be."

"I want," she replied, her mouth at his ear, making him tingle along the soles of his feet. "I'm game. I'm here."

Zane hid a smile in her shoulder, then pressed a hot but quick kiss to her neck before straightening up and reluctantly pulling back. He eyed her slowly up and down, favoring her with an approving smile. "This is golden, babe. So gorgeous, and if you hadn't come to me first, I'd have been all over you."

She grinned and curtseyed. "That was the idea." She turned her ankle to eye her boots, frowning. "I love heels, but I was told once that a tall girl should never wear heels."

"Lies," he grunted with a shake of his head. "Complete and utter lies. You wear whatever you want, and when you're with me, wear the heels. In fact, please wear them."

Mara lifted her gaze to his, her smile turning coy. "I do like the way they make my legs look." She arched in just the right way to display her leg to full and glorious effect.

He groaned with at least fourteen emotions. "So do I."

She laughed and straightened, sweeping her hands behind her back. "So. Does my boyfriend want to go grab something to eat with me?"

Zane swallowed once and held out a hand to her. "Your boyfriend would like to take his girlfriend anywhere she wants to go so long as he gets to come along."

Mara stepped forward and took his hand, her fingers easily folding between his. "Now that's where I was going." She went up a little to kiss him, though the heels rendered the distance closer than normal, which was a bonus, in his mind. "Let's get out of here."

He brought their joined hands to his lips and kissed hers softly. "You got it."

# TWELVE

OFFICIALLY HAVING A professional hockey player as a boyfriend certainly had its perks, and Mara was becoming aware of them at a shocking rate.

Having said boyfriend show up at her workplace for lunch unannounced hadn't been one she'd expected.

Not that he'd announced himself as her boyfriend when he'd gotten there or that Mara had known he'd arrived right away.

She'd simply been sitting at her desk, finishing up some documentation from the morning's clinic, when she heard the unmistakable sound of the front desk window sliding open. "Hi, can I help you?"

"Yeah, I'd like to establish myself and my daughter as new patients."

Mara's ears tingled as she perked up, the deep, delicious voice immediately giving her goosebumps. Her lips were suddenly all but buzzing as they recalled the feel of his mouth on hers, and her toes curled in her tennis shoes in response.

"With which provider?" Christina asked in her too-bright voice that she used for patients, even though she was cruel about them behind closed doors. Her fingers tapped annoyingly loud against the keyboard, and Mara tensed, knowing the girl would be blatantly checking out Zane at the window.

"Dr. Hayden."

The key tapping stopped, and Mara bit back a grin, imagining her coworker's face. Christina was the pet of Susan, followed her every wish or command, and relayed to her any information that might get anyone in the office in trouble. Yet she complained about Susan behind her back as well, so her allegiance was forever in question. She absolutely could not be trusted, and if there was one thing she was consistent in, it was that Dr. Hayden was her least favorite provider.

"Dr. Hayden?" she repeated, not bothering to hide her surprise. "He's a family doctor, sir."

"Yeah. That's why my family is setting up with him."

Mara bit back a snort of laughter, covering her mouth with both hands while leaning her elbows on her desk.

"I can understand you establishing with him, of course," Christina replied, again with the over-sincere voice. "But your daughter will want a pediatrician."

"She's five. She doesn't know what she wants," Zane said in a deadpan tone that Mara instantly loved him for.

"Right, that's not what I meant . . ."

"Look," she heard Zane huff. "I've done my homework. Dr. Hayden has been around the block, but he isn't close to retiring. He has better patient reviews than any other provider in this office, and everyone that I have spoken with just raves about him and his team. I want to set up with him, and I want my daughter to see him too."

"But . . ." Christina sputtered. "We have amazing pediatricians. Dr. Clerk alone is . . ."

"Dr. Hayden may have done a residency in family med,"

Zane overrode Christina, as he spoke louder, "but he also has a fellowship in pediatrics. I think I can safely say he is qualified to provide medical care for my little girl, wouldn't you agree?"

Christina had no response to that, and Mara would pay a lot of money to see her face right now, but there was no way she was getting involved in this moment.

"What are you laughing about?" Susan hissed as she came up to Mara's desk. "What's going on out there?"

Mara faced her office lead, forcing her expression to turn innocent. "I think someone is establishing as a new patient. I'm sorry, I was just thinking about something my dad said last night, and it made me laugh."

Susan narrowed her heavily lined eyes, her pinched expression looking even tighter against her olive complexion. It was clear she didn't quite believe Mara's lie, but she couldn't exactly find fault with what she'd said. And as there was no way to prove or disprove the statement, there was nothing she could do.

"Would you ... would you like to schedule appointments now, sir?" Christina asked, her voice strained.

"Nope, just hand me the forms I'll need, and I'll get them sent in once I have a better idea of our schedules."

Susan stepped out into the front office as Christina shuffled for papers. "You'll be very happy with our doctors here, sir. We pride ourselves on excellent patient care. Don't forget to sign up for the online portal once you establish. It makes communication so much easier."

"I bet. I've heard Dr. Hayden communicates with the patients himself rather than have a nurse do it. That's high class right there. Glad I'm going with him."

"Dr. ... Dr. Hayden. Yes, I believe he does."

Really, it sounded like Susan was choking on her words.

Mara slowly pushed up from her chair and crept over to

the wall separating her desk from the front office, leaning around just enough to get a glimpse of the front window.

Zane leaned on the counter there while he waited for the papers, denim button-up doing nothing to hide his build, his public smile in place. It was a gorgeous smile, but Mara had seen him do better.

Had been given better.

He glanced up and saw her, but his expression barely changed. His eyes said volumes, however, and Mara felt her cheeks begin a slow burn. She winked at him, then grinned as the corner of his mouth quirked.

There was no way they were going to get out of here together, even for a minute, and she had no idea what he was doing here. They had never talked about Dr. Hayden again since she'd mentioned her job in the car that night, and she'd certainly never suggested he become a patient of his.

What was his game here?

Christina finally had the paperwork and handed it all over to Zane, tossing the over-styled pouf on top of her almost pixie-cut hair as though it made anything look better. "If you change your mind on Dr. Hayden, we are happy to give you more information on any of our other providers."

Zane gave her a bland look. "I'm not changing my mind. Push me more, and I'll tell anyone who'll listen that you're biased against him, which I consider to be unprofessional behavior. I'd really hate to file a complaint before I'm officially a patient here."

Christina gasped and sat back hard against her chair.

Susan stepped forward at once. "Sir, she didn't mean anything by that. She was simply offering you . . ."

"I know what she meant," he overrode, smiling almost politely. "I just don't like being told what to do when it goes against what I want."

"I understand that, absolutely," Susan assured him in her save-this-situation voice. "We love Dr. Hayden here, I promise you that. He is such a great doctor. Have you ever been to this hospital?"

Zane straightened slowly, his smile staying put. "No, actually. I'd love to see it and hear more about the office."

Susan cleared her throat. "Mara?"

Mara stepped back quickly, only to come forward as though she'd just left her desk. "Yes?"

Susan turned to smile warmly at her, which must have hurt her features, given her true feelings. "Would you be willing to use some of your lunch to give this gentleman a tour of the hospital? He wants to become a patient of Dr. Hayden, and you are just the person to tell him all about what a wonderful provider he is and what a great experience he will have as a patient."

Oh, this was too good.

Mara kept her expression carefully composed and nodded, forcing herself to look at Zane as she would any other prospective new patients. "Of course, it would be my pleasure, sir."

"Thank you very much," Zane said with a nod, folding up the papers neatly. "So kind."

Mara smiled and turned to go back to her desk to lock her computer, only to find Susan hard on her heels.

"Recover this," Susan muttered, her eyes hard. "Don't overembellish, but keep him interested in the practice. He clearly has money, and we could use a stable patient who can afford to pay his bill in a timely matter."

"I understand," Mara replied, biting back the desire to make a retort about a patient's money being none of her business.

It wouldn't get her anywhere, and it might earn her some

snide comments, if not another round of petty retaliation in passive-aggressive ways.

Besides, this way she was getting to spend an extensive amount of time with Zane. At Susan's own request.

Checkmate, Susan.

Mara grabbed her hospital jacket and walked down the hall to the waiting room door, her heart skipping an energetic dance within her.

Last night ... after the wall moment, they'd grabbed some food and just talked while sitting in his SUV, exchanging kisses throughout. They were a thing, he'd said. And they were both in.

First sighting after such an eventful, emotional, intense evening.

When would this excitement fade? Or would it?

She stepped out into the waiting room, her fingertips tingling. Zane was casually gorgeous, berry-colored jeans working with his denim shirt beautifully, his hair covered by a white baseball cap with a black *N* on it. His scruff gave him a rugged look despite his crisp style of dressing, and his build was perfectly enhanced by all of it.

Her mouth dried, and she gestured to the doors of their department. "Shall we go?"

"Absolutely," he said with a nod, moving to the door to hold it open for her. "Lead the way."

Without looking back, they slipped out into the hall, Mara leading Zane away from the family medicine offices as though she really was leading him into the main part of the hospital. Once out of sight of the windows of her department and tucked into an abandoned hallway, however, she turned to face Zane, walking backwards and grinning at him without shame. "Are. You. Serious?"

He laughed and shrugged, tipping his hat back and

sliding his hands into his pockets. "What can I say? I have a vested interest in making sure a certain doctor succeeds, and I have no problem speaking my mind when people irritate me."

Mara shook her head, almost squealing in delight and amusement, and went to him, throwing her arms around his neck in a hug. He lifted her off the ground, still laughing, then tightened his hold as the laughter faded, sighing into her.

"What?" she murmured, folding her arms about his neck.

"Hi, baby," he replied as his hands rubbed slowly along her back. "I missed you."

Mara buried her face into his shoulder, hiding a smile. "Hi."

"I haven't kissed you today. I hate that."

She snickered and lifted her head, shivering as he lowered her very slowly to the ground, her body brushing all along his with the motion. "What are you going to do about it?"

His smile lit up every corner of her body, and he gently tipped her chin up before kissing her in the slowest, softest, most spine-tingling way known to humankind. She gripped his shirt in her hands as she tried to do something, anything, in response, but apart from breathing, she had nothing to match this.

When he broke off, she exhaled slowly, almost like she had stepped out on a wintery day and her lungs were adjusting to the temperature. "That . . . was something."

"More where that came from, but let's grab lunch." He winked and put a hand at her back, turning down another hallway. "We've got a good half hour, and I don't want to waste it up here."

"Half an hour?" Mara shot back, looking up at him in shock. "What in the world makes you think I can take a full thirty minutes away from the office? Susan would never . . ."

"Susan thinks you're in recovery mode," Zane reminded her. "And besides, I said I did my homework. You are legally entitled to a thirty-minute lunch break. If that isn't happening, it could be reported, and violators could be prosecuted, and that publicity ... yeesh." He grimaced, shaking his head. "Anyone with a decent lawyer would have it easy."

Mara laughed and slipped her arm around his waist. "I take it you have a decent lawyer?"

Zane pulled her tight into his side, crooked smile in place. "I have an amazing lawyer. He gets the best presents out of anyone on my Christmas list, family included."

"Good to know." She looked up at him, surprised at how comfortable walking with him like this was. "How was breakfast with Jax?"

"Great," came the easy reply. "He was upset you weren't there, since he really wanted to meet you officially, but he was really happy to see Hope." He shook his head with a reluctant smile. "She really loves her uncle Jax. No clue why."

"That's adorable," Mara said with a laugh. "She has all these big tough hockey players wrapped around her finger."

Zane chuckled in response as they reached the stairs and began to head down them. "It's true; she could get anything she wanted from any of us. Easily. Maybe not Trane, he's a tough nut to crack, but he still turns soft around her."

Mara smiled at the imagery, remembering the huge goalie Zane had pointed out the night they'd watched the game together. She had no idea what he really looked like or how he behaved, but by size alone she was amused by the possibilities. It was easy to imagine Hope winning over anyone, even impressive guys like her father. Mara loved the girl herself, and part of her attraction to Zane was his fatherhood and how much it meant to him.

How much it was a part of him.

How much Hope adored him.

Attractive as Zane was just by sight, seeing that part of him was that much more appealing.

As if he needed the help.

"Do you have plans for Hope's birthday?" Mara asked as the two of them entered the hospital cafeteria. "I know she's pretty set on one of those stuffed animals."

"Don't remind me," he muttered, trying to look gruff even though he smiled. "The price tag outweighs my indulgence."

Mara snickered as she stepped away from him to grab a tray. "Why do I doubt that?"

He coughed in mock distress, following her with a tray of his own. "I beg your pardon, Mara Matthews, but have you seen anything in my house that indicates I spoil my daughter?"

He had a point there; for all the money he must have made with his career, his house was fairly simple. Nice, comfortable, but nothing to indicate that he was a professional athlete making a fortune.

"Well, I don't know," she protested, batting away a hand of his that had wandered to her hip. "I haven't seen Hope's room or her . . . what did you call it? Imagination Station?"

Zane laughed at her amused confusion. "That's the name, yeah. Josie just calls it Hope's cubby, but there's a room on the second floor that we converted into a playroom, and she has a mini office in there. Creative stuff there, art supplies and the like. My mom and Rae put it together for her when she turned four. If I ever can't find Hope, chances are she is there."

"A mini office," Mara repeated as she started assembling a salad for herself. "And you expect me to believe she isn't spoiled."

"It's not like she has a Jeep." Zane bypassed the salad,

going around Mara to the rest of the buffet. "And I didn't do it; the grandmas did."

Mara shook her head, piling more toppings onto her salad. "Do you know how incredible and unheard of it is that your mom and stepmom do things together?"

Zane exhaled a chuckle, reaching for a second roll. "I do know, I've heard it all before, trust me. Mom and Rae go to the same book club. Dad and Wayne are golf buddies. Now, I know they haven't always gotten along, but they never let that trickle down to us kids. We always came first."

"I imagine that affected how you parent Hope," Mara murmured, sliding her tray closer as she reached for a roll herself.

"Sure. She comes first and last, the end." He shrugged a shoulder. "Being an athlete can be a pretty public career, though I can't pretend hockey players get the same attention as some other guys." He made a face of pretended exasperation before grinning at her. "But that actually works out well for me. A few of my teammates know about Hope, since I'll bring her to the family activities the Hounds organization puts on, but otherwise, there isn't much to tie us together. I want to protect her from the publicity, if that makes sense."

It *did* make sense, and more than that, Mara was touched by it. Some guys might use their single-dad status as an improvement in their dating prospects, but Zane was a father first, single second.

Well, not as single now as he had been a few weeks ago, but still.

"How often does Hope get to see your family?" Mara asked as they moved away from the buffet to the cashiers. "You mentioned they're still in Chicago."

He nodded, tugging a credit card out of his wallet and gesturing that he was paying for both trays. "They come out for a couple of games every season, if they can. Every time I play Chicago, they're there. We've been in Chicago a little more in the last few months, so that's been fun. We're going back next weekend for a Northbrook event..."

Mara frowned as he trailed off, nudging him with her elbow. "Yeah? And?"

He turned to face her, his eyes wide, a small smile curving one side of his mouth. "Come with us."

She blinked in response, wondering why thought was suddenly difficult. "Do what now?"

He took a step closer to her, smile growing. "Come with us. To Chicago, to the event, everything. Come."

"Zane, I can't," she told him, laughing in disbelief. "I have work, and you don't need me tagging along with you and Hope, especially with your family and your Northbrook friends..."

"I'm serious," he insisted, putting a hand on her arm and squeezing gently. "I want you there. I want you with me."

Her heart made a strange keening sound that only she could hear, and it was as though her stomach fluttered. She wanted to be with him, wherever he was, whatever he was doing, but admitting that to herself was terrifying.

She'd been in this relationship for days. Officially, not even one, but unofficially just a few.

The phrase *head over heels* had always seemed strange to her and hadn't made sense, but now that was exactly how she felt. Flipping end over end in the air, dizzy with exhilaration and all consumed by the experience.

She could drown in all of this. In Zane.

Happily.

But should she?

"I..."

"Sir?"

They turned to look at the cashier, who was holding out Zane's credit card expectantly, expression bland and bored.

Zane smiled anyway and took the card from her. "Thank you. Have a great day." He tilted his head towards a table, and Mara followed, exhaling slowly.

Could she go to Chicago with him? It felt like he would be introducing her to his family, and it had to be too soon for that, right? He wouldn't want to do that this early in their relationship, right?

She didn't want to rush into anything, right?

"Madam?" Zane intoned, gesturing grandly to the table he'd set the tray on. "May I help you with your chair?"

Mara rolled her eyes with a laugh and moved to the seat. "Oh, why not?"

He performed his role with perfection, sliding her chair out and pushing it in with impeccable timing. He stooped behind her and pressed a surprisingly heated kiss just beneath her right ear, making her jump and shiver in the same breath and bite back a moan on the next.

*RUSH!* her inner voice screamed desperately, and her hormones applauded the idea.

Zane sat in his own chair across from her and winked, clearly knowing exactly what he'd just done to her.

"Not nice," Mara scolded, digging into her salad.

"I don't know, I thought it was very nice." He shrugged as he cut into his roast beef. "So. Chicago."

Mara gave him a look, chewing quickly. "I need to think about it. Taking a trip together this soon seems fast."

He nodded at that. "I can see that, sure. But this is a trip I'm already taking, and Hope is coming too. We might celebrate her birthday while we're there, and now that we are what we are . . ."

That made her smile, wondering just what he thought they were. She cocked her head, eyes narrowing.

One of his feet pressed down on her toes beneath the

table, and she almost hiccupped on her next bite of salad. "I just think it would be more fun with you there," he finished in the same simple tone as before.

Mara considered that, her fork fiddling around with more salad. "How formal is the event?"

"Not very. I'll be in a suit, and I think the guys will too, but like a casual suit. Church-barbecue suit, not wedding suit."

"When was the last time you were at a church barbecue?" Mara laughed, clapping her hands once as she sat back against her chair. "Oh lands, Zane..."

His foot pressed down against hers with a steadily increasing force. "I love your laugh," he murmured, his eyes on her mouth. "Such a great sound. We need more of that in our lives."

"Laughter?" That surprised her; Hope was constantly laughing, and Zane had one of the best senses of humor she'd found in a guy. They were happy together, and they laughed together.

What more could they want?

Zane shook his head slowly. "*Your* laughter, babe. You have no idea what it feels like to hear it." He reached out and took her hand across the table, his thumb rubbing over the surface of her skin in a tantalizing way. "Think about Chicago, okay? No pressure, it's not make or break, I would just really love for you to come. See where I learned to skate. Meet the guys. Meet my insane family, if you can handle that much."

There was no helping the snickering at that, especially considering the fond smile he wore in conjunction with eyes wide with meaning.

Why couldn't she just leap? What was stopping her from tossing it all to the wind and going with this fun, gorgeous, caring, remarkably normal-acting guy to his hometown?

"And it would make Hope's birthday," he added, his thumb still brushing her skin. "She's already told me you're invited to her birthday. The whole day. Whatever we do."

Mara groaned and made a face. "That's not fair, and you know it."

"I'm not making it up, but I won't pretend I wouldn't love it too." He winked again and released her tingling hand. "Hope seriously thinks you're the greatest."

"The feeling is mutual." Mara smiled at him, then brightened. "Hey! You have a game tomorrow, and Hope said she's never seen you play for real. I could bring her. No one would know she's yours, and she'd get the fun experience of watching her daddy do his thing!"

Zane didn't really react, but his eyes stayed on her, his smile remaining small.

"Is that a terrible idea?" Mara asked, her nose wrinkling. "It's a terrible idea, huh? You don't want her exposed to all that, and it's probably too loud and crazy, and way past her bedtime . . ."

"I think it's a great idea," Zane interrupted softly.

"You do?"

He nodded, the motion slow and somehow full of heat. "I love that you thought of it. Thought of her. Want to do it. I love it, Mara. More than that, I think Hope will love it."

Mara smiled almost shyly, her cheeks heating. "You do?" she asked again.

He reached for her hand again, this time lacing their fingers together. "Yeah. I do."

There was something magical about holding his hand, and there weren't really words for it.

There didn't need to be.

Mara sighed and looked at a clock on the wall. "Yikes. Twenty more minutes, and then I need to get back."

"Tell Susan you won me over."

"You want me to lie to my office lead?" Mara laughed.

"Not a lie," Zane told her, his fingers brushing against hers. "You have. Completely."

Mara gave him a look. "Zane. Do you want me to be able to focus at all the rest of the day?"

"Not really, no."

The casual admission made her snort a laugh, which sent them both laughing, and the next twenty minutes went by much faster than either of them wanted.

# THIRTEEN

"Yes, Hopey, it is okay if you have french fries tonight. You are going to have so much fun with Mara tonight."

"I know that, silly," Hope giggled through the phone. "Mara is the bestest person *ever*."

Zane laughed at the conviction in his daughter's voice as he got out of his SUV. "She's pretty special, huh?"

"The specialest. Will you wave at me tonight, Daddy?"

"You bet, pumpkin. Watch for the signal, okay?"

"Okay. Bye, Daddy. Have a good show."

Zane chuckled again and nodded. "Always do. Bye, Dopey." Shaking his head, he slid his phone into his back pocket. He hefted his bag over his shoulder and started towards the arena, only to feel a buzzing in his pocket.

He grinned, wondering what Hope had forgotten to ask him now, and reached back to retrieve the phone. One look at the screen wiped the smile from his face.

*Michelle.*

He exhaled slowly before hitting the answer button. "Hello?"

"Hi, Zane."

It was astonishing how unchanged her voice was after all this time and all they had been through. He remembered when the sound of it could make him smile and feel at home.

It hadn't had that effect in a long time.

Now it only tightened his stomach and made him grouchy. "Michelle."

"I've been calling."

"I know," he clipped with a nod. "No messages, so I didn't see a need to call back."

There was a sigh from the other end of the line. "Fair enough. You have a minute?"

"Not really," he replied. He nodded at the security guy at the players' entrance as he walked through, and turned down the corridor towards the locker room. "We have a game tonight, I just got to the arena."

"Then you do have a minute. I remember how early you like to get there."

Her tone turned warm, almost fond when she said that, and it sent a shiver of awareness up his spine, his hair standing on end. "What do you want, Michelle? We called you three months ago for your birthday, and you sent us to voicemail."

"My phone was off."

"It rang twice and then went," Zane shot back, forcing a harsh exhale in the hopes it would contain his temper. "That's an intentional send."

"Okay, so I didn't want to take the call," Michelle admitted, surprising him. "I was partying with my friends on my birthday."

Zane nodded and leaned against the wall outside of the locker room. "Figured. So what do you want?"

She hesitated, but nothing about that hesitation would raise Zane's curiosity. There were no visits coming up, nothing for Michelle to complain about, and no one was expecting her to call or send a card for Hope's birthday next week. She had shown the quality of her parenting a long time ago.

"I want to terminate my parental rights."

For a full three heartbeats, Zane's heart didn't, in fact, beat. He blinked once, the pressure of the wall at his back the only thing keeping him upright. Michelle was a lousy co-parent, but he had always assumed it was a phase and that someday she would grow up and see what she had.

He hadn't expected this.

Ever.

"Michelle," he managed harshly, "there's no coming back from that. Once it's done, it's done. You know that, right?"

"Of course I know that, did you think I would go into this without talking with my lawyer?" The spite he had expected her voice to hold was finally evident, and it raised his hackles.

"How is Greg?" Zane asked with a sneer. "Did he get that divorce you claimed you wanted?"

He could almost hear her snarl. "Don't be petty. Greg isn't my lawyer anymore, and you have no right to accuse me of anything. I don't claim alimony anymore, and I pay child support."

Zane barked a hard laugh. "Thirty bucks when you remember isn't child support. You're lucky I haven't sent the courts after you. I'm surprised your new lawyer hasn't instructed you to fix that yet."

"The point is, Zane," Michelle replied without replying, "that I can't file for termination without someone to step in as a mother figure for the kid on a permanent basis. Illinois frowns on leaving a child without two parents."

"Imagine that. And her name is Hope, remember?" He looked up at the ceiling, shaking his head, his eyes tracing over the rivets and bolts there without real interest. "So I need to get remarried for you to get what you want."

"Pretty much. But if I show a pattern of neglect, they may find me in contempt and grant a temporary stay of visitation."

Zane exhaled a snort, closing his eyes. "That's supposed to be disciplinary, Michelle, not a guideline."

"Look, you want me out of her life, and I want out of her life. This is a win-win."

"You listen to me," Zane snarled, his eyes popping open, turning so his back would face any incoming teammates. "I have *never* wanted you out of Hope's life. Ever. I have bent over backwards to keep you in it. The only reason I have not shown up at your front door with Hope at my side is that you keep moving and I don't know where you are."

"It's better that way," Michelle assured him. "I'm not a mom."

"Not wanting to be a mom is not the same as erasing being a mom." He pinched the bridge of his nose with a sigh. "Nothing about my baby girl losing her mom is a win, okay?"

He heard Michelle sigh, and he heard the finality in it. "I'm not her mom, Zane. That's what I'm trying to tell you. I gave birth to her, and that is all. I'm sorry, but I want out. Completely."

Zane's throat clenched, and for a moment, he couldn't breathe.

"And can you tell my dad to stop visiting?" she went on. "It's really awkward for me."

"I'm not telling your dad a damn thing," Zane informed her. "He is more than welcome in her life. If you want him to be out too, you can tell him."

"Fine. I'll call him next."

Zane swore softly, squeezing his eyes shut for just a moment. Swallowing hard, he shook his head. "Please don't do this," he begged. "Please."

"It's done," she said softly. "I've already filed my intentions on the off chance I find a sympathetic judge."

"Sympathetic to child abandonment?" Zane snapped. "Not a chance."

"I want a new life, Zane. A free life."

"You've already made it new and free."

"I know. You and the kid are the last shackles holding me back."

Zane turned and banged a fist against the cement wall, every muscle in his body tensing. "Shackles," he repeated. "Our daughter is a shackle to you. How can you say that?"

"Leave it alone, Zane. As soon as conditions are right, I'm taking you to court and ending this once and for all. And please stop having her call me. I won't answer."

"Her name is Hope," Zane ground out, his fist thumping the wall softly as the tension in his chest turned vicelike. "Why can't you even say her name? What is wrong with you?"

"Goodbye, Zane. My lawyer will be in touch."

There was silence as the call ended, and it was all Zane could do to avoid attempting to crush the phone in his hand.

How could she? *How* could she?

He unclenched his hand from his phone and put it back in his pocket with careful motions. Pushing off the wall, he moved further down the hall, leaving his bag where it was, and continued moving until he found an open storage room. He let himself in, glancing around at the out-of-date practice gear and metal chairs in the early stages of rusting.

Perfect.

With a roar of rage and indignation, Zane picked up the nearest chair, throwing it across the room. He kicked at piles of shoulder and chest pads, picked up two warped hockey sticks and beat them against the floor until they broke, and slammed another chair against the wall so many times his ears began to ring. He dropped the chair to the floor with a clatter of sound and stared around at the destruction, though he hadn't done as much as he wanted.

Sanity poked at his rage, reminding him that there was a game coming up and he needed to be careful.

Opportunity chimed in that he was an enforcer on the ice and hitting people was his job.

Satisfaction grinned maliciously and turned Zane on his heel, striding out of the closet.

Three of his teammates stood at the locker room door, wide-eyed and staring at him as he came towards them.

"You okay in there, Z?" Avery asked, the headphones around his neck blaring music.

Zane nodded, the energy within him coiling and building further still. "Letting off steam before we hit the ice."

Ramsey raised a brow. "Not saving it *for* the ice?"

"Gotta get rid of some," Zane explained with a grim smile, "or I won't be on the ice that long at all."

Javvy grinned at him, nodding in appreciation. "Gonna light 'em up today, huh?"

"Oh yeah." Zane picked up his bag and followed the trio into the locker room. "Big time."

Less than an hour later, he was out on the ice with his team, warming up for the game and letting the feel of the ice beneath his blades fill him with a sense of certainty and confidence. He circled their zone again and again, shifting to skate backwards a few times without any dramatic flair that he might have added at any other time. Tonight wasn't about drama or a show. It was about lighting up the enemy and making them pay.

At the moment, in lieu of the real target of his anger, the enemy was the Carolina Cyclones.

Anybody would understand that, under the circumstances. The Pit certainly would. He'd texted them with very brief details the moment he'd gone into the locker room, and their responses were epic.

*Trane: [insert many colorful profanities I'm saying out loud]*

*Rocco: What he said.*

*Clint: There is a very special circle of hell for some people.*

*Dice: That's ridiculous. I mean absolutely ridiculous. Who needs her? We're Hope's family now.*

Every single one of them had liked that comment, and Zane would freely admit to being choked up at it.

Then Jax had capped it all.

*Jax: Her birthday is Saturday, right? Let's give her a party. After the Northbrook thing, it's Hope's night. Can we break her curfew, Dad?*

He'd had to go out to the ice after that, but he knew he'd have a ton of messages waiting for him.

Hope had an army at her back. There was some consolation in that.

He craned his neck from side to side, avoiding his usual pregame antics with his teammates as well. He took a few shots on goal, shuffled the puck around with a couple of players, but for the most part said nothing. He needed the fury within him to remain contained but lose none of its intensity. He needed to harness it in preparation for the right moments.

He needed to be Zamboni tonight in every respect.

"Javvy says you're on fire already," Shap said as he suddenly appeared at Zane's side.

He only grunted in response.

"Just remember you can't get a fifth penalty," his captain went on. "Four is fine. Five, no bueno."

Zane frowned and looked over at the lanky winger. "I'm well aware of the penalty restrictions of a single game, Shap. Why are you telling me?"

Shap shrugged his shoulders, tapping his stick on the ice.

"Don't want to lose you for the whole game. I don't mind you lighting them up, just don't get tossed out."

In an unprecedented move, Zane grinned at Shap without hesitation. "Are you giving me permission to go hard, O captain?"

"Do your thing, Zamboni." Shap returned his smile. "Make it a good game." He pushed off and scooped up the puck, heading for the goal in a practice shot.

"Yes, sir." Zane shook his head, then forced the smile back. There was nothing to be gained from smiling on the ice, unless he was looking to unnerve someone.

That was always a fun move.

He bounced slightly on his skates, shaking his arms and legs to loosen them further, craning his neck one more time. This game needed to get started, and he needed to get at it.

He looked up at the stands, skating around in small circles now, just for the sake of keeping moving and to not lose momentum. It would be hard to spot Mara and Hope in a crowd this size, but as he remembered, his tickets were always . . .

He bit back a smile at the sight of a tall brunette with amazing legs in skinny jeans coming down the stairs towards a section, her hand holding that of a girl with bouncing pigtails. Both wore black T-shirts, the Hounds logo emblazoned in gold, though the little girl's was glittery and glinted in the arena lights. And her shoes were bright pink.

The sight of his baby girl at once filled him with joy and agony. That angel had a mother who no longer wanted to be considered such in any sense of the word. That sweet girl was being intentionally neglected by a parent.

He was officially all that she had in the world.

And that lit a fire in him that nothing else could.

*We're her family now.*

The reminder of the Pit's claim on his daughter settled him just enough to let sanity return.

Hope saw him and waved, tugging Mara's hand and pointing. Mara looked, and he could barely see her grin. She blew him a subtle kiss, then turned to go into the seats, but Hope kept her attention on Zane.

He stared right back, swallowing hard. He tapped his helmet once, then his heart, then his head again, before putting his fingers to his mouth.

Her smile could have lit the arena all by itself.

He would play for her tonight. Avenge her wrongs, if it could be done by proxy, and protect her from any and all threats. Suddenly, every opponent on the ice was on the side of his ex-wife and saw Hope as nothing more than an inconvenience.

Returning his focus to the ice, Zane exhaled slowly through his nose, a quiet fire simmering in his gut. He followed his teammates off the ice, barely hearing their pep talk, barely aware of skating back out when he was introduced, and barely seeing the puck drop in the faceoff.

But the moment that puck hit the ice, he was on.

He checked a Cyclones winger into the boards in the first minute of the game, the hit clean, and the puck safely swept to his own line.

Shadowing his forwards, Zane hovered, his eyes catching every flick of the puck and position of the orange-jersey-wearing Cyclones. He got a cleared puck and sent it to Boomer for safety before blocking a winger from getting closer to it. Janny fumbled a charge to the goal, and Zane retreated to the goal with a muffled curse as the Cyclones turned the tables on them.

"Hot! Hot! Hot!" he bellowed, though his wingers were already scrambling to get back to him.

Zane swept to his left, engaging the puck carrier head on, when the puck moved to his right, just as Zane hoped it would. He charged towards the forward, picking up speed as he did so, and crushed him hard into the boards, only belatedly going after the puck at his feet. He barely got it free enough for Janny to break away with it.

Zane followed, leaving the beleaguered Cyclones winger behind, then turned and flattened another coming behind Janny.

The whistle blew, and Zane rolled his eyes.

"Interference," the ref called. "Two minutes."

"Really?" Zane barked at him. "Really?"

The ref pointed at the box, and Zane waved a dismissive arm at him, shaking his head as he skated to the box.

The crowd booed their agreement.

Zane sat moodily and watched the clock tick down. His left knee bounced with agitation, his eyes tracking every play and movement of the puck. He rose to his feet frequently, calling out to his teammates, who were doing a decent job of containing the powerplay. But that couldn't last forever.

He needed to be out there.

The penalty finally wound down, and Zane was released, charging out of the box headlong and making a beeline for the right winger, currently carrying the puck towards the Hounds goal.

Their collision was a thing of beauty and without any possible penalty call as Zane slammed into him. The action knocked him off course and off his feet, sending the puck harmlessly to Pike, who swept it around the goal to Boomer so he could take it safely up ice.

The Hounds line took the puck from him, and with a quick succession of great puck movements, a goal was scored.

Zane exhaled in relief and swept back around to his

starting position. The crowd was amped up, and usually he would have encouraged them with gestures to bring it up or with fist pumps. This time, he only nodded at them all.

It seemed to do the trick well enough, and the noise went up another notch.

The music leaking through the speakers of the arena added to the energy, the beat pounding hard in Zane's ears. It drowned out all possible distraction and returned his focus to center ice.

The Hounds won the faceoff and fiddled around in the Cyclones' zone without making much progress. Zane and Boomer switched off the ice and cheered on their team until the buzzer signaled the end of the first period. Zane headed off the ice with his teammates, wishing the next seventeen minutes would fly by.

Thankfully, his wish was granted, and it seemed like only moments later that he was switching back out onto the ice, shortly after the Hounds had scored another goal. He had a couple of great hits, ones that lit the crowd up, and none that had him sent to the penalty box.

Then one of the wingers took a cheap shot at Kelso that wasn't called, and Zane felt his less sportsmanlike attitude come out. He swept around, hovering as he waited for the next opportunity, and found himself grinning slowly as the Cyclones were making another press for goal. Zane pushed forward as they shuttled the puck among themselves, and he lowered his shoulder to ram into the offending Cyclones winger from behind, sending the smaller player flying to the ice.

Two Cyclones players rushed at him in revenge, but Zane avoided any and all intention of fighting with them. One penalty would be enough, and as far as he was concerned, the score was settled.

The ref called the penalty for crosschecking, and this time Zane made no attempt to fight it. He knew full well what his penalty was, and he was fine with it. This time he did give the crowd behind the penalty box a cocky grin, and they roared their approval. He sat in the box with more of his usual swagger and attitude, though he wouldn't commit fully to it. He wasn't drumming up penalties for his own amusement this time.

This was his version of coping and therapy.

Very cathartic.

Five minutes in the box felt much longer than seventeen minutes in the locker room at intermission had, but at least he felt better about it.

A good hit was worth appreciating.

The powerplay finally ended, and he was free to return to the ice. The front line switched out for a new shift, and Zane hovered protectively on his side of center ice, forcing him to cool off just enough to keep from wasting game time. His hits were hard, and he would have a few more before the night was out, but there was no sense in using them all up before the third period started. Something needed to be a finale.

Besides, he was more than just a great hitter.

He met a Cyclones player at the boards, scuffling for the puck and tapping it away before chasing after it, falling back when one of his own players took it forward. He moved up the further the play moved and kept the puck in play when the Cyclones attempted to clear it. A brazen charge by the Cyclones center, playing on fresh legs, caught them all off guard and sent Zane backpedaling almost frantically to get in a better position.

Boomer suddenly streaked across his field of vision, crashing hard into the center with enough force that the cracking sound of it made a general moan rise up from the crowd. Ramsey dropped back to carry the puck up the boards, racing it out of danger, and Boomer, whooping at the lack of call, followed him as shadow as far as he could.

"That was close," Zane muttered to himself, hunching over as he inched forward, his eyes tracking the play. He glanced over his left shoulder at Pike, who tapped his helmet with his stick in an almost salute.

Zane nodded back, then looked at the play again. He counted quickly, frowning, then heard a commotion to his right.

The Cyclones player Boomer had hit still lay on the ice, not moving. The fans near him had only just noticed and were beginning to call out about it.

Zane swore and raced over to him. "Hey!" he bellowed, waving at the refs. "Hey! Hey!"

He heard a whistle blow as he reached the player, scrambling in his mind for the name as he dropped to his knees. "Breckin. Breckin, can you hear me?"

The player lay there, eyes open, staring up at nothing, though he seemed to be breathing.

"Breckin," Zane said again, knowing better than to touch him as Breckin's teammates started to come to them. "Hang on, buddy. Medics are headed out." He turned and waved frantically, grunting with approval as Kelso ushered the athletic trainer out to them and Boomer had their doc.

Zane scooted out of the way when they arrived, and he skated over to Pike at the goal, who had straightened fully and pushed back his mask. "I didn't even see him," Pike muttered, squirting the water from his water bottle into his mouth.

"No one did," Zane reminded him. "Killer hit, and the play moved so fast." He shook his head, then gestured for water, which Pike squirted into his mouth for him. "It's not good, Pike. The kid isn't responsive."

Pike hissed as he grimaced. "That sucks. He's gonna be all-star good in about two years if this isn't it."

Zane nodded, watching as the medics brought the stretcher out on the ice. Some of the Cyclones in the box had their heads lowered, and even some of the Hounds were doing the same. No matter who the player was, no matter whom he played for, no one wanted to see this.

The medical staff seemed to have some trouble figuring out how to lift Breckin onto the stretcher on the ice with the numbers they had. Without thinking, Zane skated over.

"Can I help?" he offered, putting a hand on the shoulder of the nearest Cyclones player, who had also come forward.

The player turned to him, a *C* on his jersey, a relieved smile on his face. "That'd be great, Z."

Zane nodded and patted his shoulder, then looked at the doctor. "Where do you need me, doc?"

The doctor gave them all clear instructions, and they carefully lifted Breckin onto the stretcher. Zane was glad to see the kid responding now, though his words were slurred and he wasn't making much sense. The medical team strapped him down, then hurried him off the ice to the applause of the crowd.

Zane skated over to center ice, where the captain and another player watched their teammate leave the ice. "You guys good?"

They nodded, one of them shrugging. "Doesn't look great, but it's out of our hands. We'll play our hearts out for him."

Boomer skated over to them, looking a little shaken. "Hey, I told Breckin on his way out, but I'm not sure he'll remember it. I didn't mean to hit him that hard, definitely didn't mean to hurt him. I'm really sorry, guys."

The captain reached over and patted Boomer's back

twice. "No sweat, Boomer. We're good. Any of my guys that aren't good, they'll hear it from me."

Boomer nodded, then he and Zane skated back to their position, a little quieter than they had been earlier. "I hate when that happens," Boomer muttered.

"Agreed." Zane cleared his throat and turned to face center ice again. "Like he said, though. Out of our hands now. Let's light 'em up."

# FOURTEEN

AT WHAT POINT did the shaking of one's hands become something to worry about?

It had been five days, and both of Mara's hands still trembled at the memory of the hockey player that had been carted off of the ice. She had dreamed about it every night since, only the face she saw on the player each time belonged to Zane. Waking up had brought relief and panic in equal measure, but it was the two times she hadn't woken up immediately that scared her most.

Dramatic medical procedural shows hadn't done her any favors in her life, if the turn of those two particular dreams was anything to go by.

She hadn't told Zane about the dreams yet, given that he'd been away with the team and played games three out of the five nights he'd been gone.

Tonight they were going out, though he wouldn't tell her where and had only said to meet him at the park. Waiting there now, Mara was afraid she'd put a strange spin on things if she flung herself on Zane and refused to let go. She needed to see him alive, well, and whole. She had watched every single minute of every single game and texted him immediately after each one, breathlessly waiting for him to respond.

He always did, and as far as she could tell, he hadn't suspected her panic.

Her fear over his potential and completely hypothetical injury startled her—particularly the depth of that fear. It consumed her thoughts, her emotions, and, as evidenced by her current tremors, her hands.

She couldn't lose Zane. Couldn't see him hurt. Couldn't bear the thought of either.

The intensity of those feelings terrified her. It was so fast, so soon, and so much . . . *so* much. Way more than she'd ever felt for any other guy in her life. But was that because she was afraid, or was the fear evidence of her feelings?

Seeing Zane would tell her that. She would know how she felt and what to do moving forward where they were concerned.

Spending time with Hope while Zane had been gone had been good for her, mostly because she knew Hope had been just as afraid about the injury they had witnessed as Mara had been. She'd turned to her with wide eyes and asked if her daddy was going to get hurt like that too. Mara had been able to convince her that it wouldn't happen, that her dad played hockey every day and never got hurt like that, but the question hadn't left Mara's mind since then.

She doubted that Andrew Breckin had been hurt like that before or that anyone would think he'd have to be carted off the ice like that. He would have had years of experience of *not* being seriously injured to go off of, just like Zane did. His family would have lived some version of Mara's dream, though she had heard that he would make a full recovery, despite his season being done.

She needed to see Zane. She needed to hold Zane, and she needed Zane to hold her.

She wouldn't be okay until he did.

"Hello, beautiful."

The low, warm purr rippled across her skin like rays of sunshine, and Mara turned towards it, a sob and gasp combining in her throat. "Zane!"

His crooked grin was there, and he eyed her up and down with the sort of heated surveyance every woman had ever dreamed of. "I don't know how you did it, but somehow you became more perfect while I was gone."

The flattery caught her square in the chest, and she felt her eyes begin to burn with tears. She reached for his face and crushed her lips to his, arching into him with a feverous energy suddenly screeching through her. How had five days felt so much longer?

Zane's arms were instantly around her, though he wasn't matching her in the almost frantic way she was attacking him. At all. He seemed to be trying to slow things down, draw things out, maybe even rein her in, yet he wasn't stopping anything. One of his hands ran up and down her back in a slow, steady cadence, and Mara could feel herself relaxing into him.

"Baby," he murmured as he finally broke away. He smoothed his thumb over her cheek, meeting her eyes and somehow seeing everything. "Not that I didn't love that, surprising as it was, but that was intense, even for us. What's going on? You okay?"

How had he known so soon? Mara was a terrible liar, it was true, but she hadn't said anything at all.

"I missed you," she whispered, leaning into him, her brow touching his chin. "And I'm sorry."

His arms wrapped around her again, holding her snuggly against him. "Sorry for missing me? Sweetheart, I missed you too, there's nothing to be sorry about."

Her heart fluttered at his admission. "No," she murmured as she swallowed, needing to get this out. "I'm sorry that I took Hope to a game where someone was seriously hurt. It's all she talked about that night, and she brings it up every time I see her now." Tears welled in Mara's eyes, even behind her closed lids, and she slid her hands down from Zane's neck, gripping his shirt. "I'm so sorry. Your daughter is afraid of your job because of me."

"Mara," Zane soothed gently, his hands moving along her spine again. "That is not your fault. Injuries happen in hockey. They happen all the time. Not always that bad, but they do happen. Hope was going to see a bad one sooner or later."

Mara shook her head against him. "But it had to be the one I took her to. It feels like my fault. It's my fault she's scared to have you play hockey now."

Zane sighed a laugh, pressing his lips against her hairline. "Baby, last week she was scared of bedbugs because she learned what they are. It's fine."

She reared back, frowning at him. "Bedbugs and getting carted off the ice on a stretcher are not the same thing!"

"No," he agreed slowly, "they're not. Sounds like Hope isn't the only one scared of my job."

Mara exhaled shakily, gripping his shirt in her hands as the memories rushed back in. "I thought I was going to be sick the entire time I watched the medical staff work on him. I know just enough to scare myself with that stuff, if that makes sense. I wasn't seeing Andrew Breckin on that stretcher, I saw you, and that . . ." She shuddered, which prompted Zane to pull her in closer.

She let him, resting her head on him and sliding her arms around him. "I could barely make it through any of your other games after that. I did, but barely. Every time you got hit, or you hit someone, I expected you to be badly hurt. I feel like an idiot; I told Hope you play hockey all the time and never get hurt, but the reality is . . . you could. You really could, and even though I know you probably won't, I can't let go of that fear."

"Sweetheart . . ." Zane's voice rumbled in his chest, reverberating against her and sending warm shivers through her. "Would you like to know how many season-ending injuries I have had in my career?"

"None?" she offered dryly, though she really didn't want to know.

"Five," he said simply.

Mara looked up at him in confusion. "Five? Really?"

He nodded, giving her a soft, crooked smile. "Two in peewee, two in high school, one my rookie season. I bounced back. You're in medicine, babe, you know how recovery works. They fix us up, we work hard, and we get back to it. It's not fun, but it's part of the job. My buddy Clint was in the Marines for a few years, and now he plays for St. Louis. Do you think his job now is as dangerous as his job then?"

"The comparison doesn't matter," Mara insisted. "It's just . . ." She swallowed hard. "I don't want to lose you."

Zane's eyes widened, and he brought one hand to Mara's jaw. "You aren't going to lose me. Ever. Not on the ice, not in real life, not anywhere. I'm healthy, I'm strong, and I'm safe. I'm not going anywhere, okay?"

Mara nodded, her eyes filling with tears.

"Okay?" he pressed again, his thumb brushing away a tear that had fallen.

"Okay," she whispered.

Zane nodded, then pressed his lips to her brow, holding her close to him. His lips dusted softly across her hairline, but without any real pattern or direction. Delightfully soothing and almost ticklish though it was, it didn't seem to be part of any PDA that might be on his agenda. It was more absent, more comforting.

More distracting.

Mara tested a theory, tugging herself just a little closer, and Zane obliged, increasing his hold, his lips still at her hair. He didn't say a word; he just held her.

Or was she holding him?

"What's wrong?" Mara murmured.

The fact that he didn't immediately put off her concern seemed significant. "Something's come up," he said in a low, tight voice. "I've been working on it for days, and it's not getting better. I don't know if I should . . . if you would . . ." He exhaled shortly, pressing his lips against her hair with more intent for a second. "I don't know what to do, Mara, and I don't know if I want you in all of this."

Something in her chest tightened, and not exactly with pleasure. "Why?"

"I'm worried it will scare you off," he admitted, something in his voice almost giving out, which weakened her knees in an instant. "That you won't want . . . I need . . . I want to tell you everything, but if it . . ."

Mara's tears renewed at his hesitation, and she pulled back with a sniff, taking his face in her hands, meeting his eyes. "I'm right here," she told him with as much strength as she could muster. "Not going to run. Not easy to scare. If you need something from me, Zane, I'll give it, if I'm able to." She went up on her toes to kiss him softly, for once not intending to start something.

Zane pressed one of his hands against hers, turning his face to kiss her palm, then laced their fingers together. "Okay."

Smiling as gently as possible, Mara tugged on his hand and led him over to a nearby bench. She sat and patted the spot beside her, which Zane took, surprising her by not sitting closer or putting his arm around the back of the bench. Instead he leaned forward, elbows on his knees, looking out at the pond in front of them as the colors of sunset faded from it, the lights of the park winking on.

Mara tucked her hand between his arm and his body, wrapping her fingers loosely around his arm, if for no other reason than to maintain contact with him, and waited.

"I got a call from Michelle the other day," Zane began, his voice rough and sounding as though it scraped through his throat. "I thought she was going to complain about scheduled visitation again and say she couldn't make it work. She always does that. I'd say that nothing she does surprises me anymore, but she got me good this time."

Questions rose and swirled around Mara in a frenzy, but she bit them all back, sensing she needed to just let Zane talk. He knew that she was here and that she was listening. That just might be enough.

He swallowed hard. "She told me . . . she told me that she wants to voluntarily terminate her parental rights."

The night was instantly colder, and Mara would have sworn birds stopped singing. "What?" she whispered, ignoring her plan to stay silent.

Zane didn't seem to hear her. "I didn't think she knew what that meant or what it entailed, but she's actually done some digging, and I got the paperwork from her lawyer. Intention to forfeit parental rights, it says. Can't be filed yet, the state of Illinois doesn't like to grant this sort of thing without a contingent parental figure to step in."

Mara's cheeks flamed at the image her mind conjured, her fingers brushing against Zane's arm anxiously as she scooted closer.

"She doesn't want to be Hope's mom," Zane went on. "At

all. In any way. Doesn't want Hope to call, doesn't want to see her ... couldn't even call our daughter by her name." He rubbed his hands over his face, then lowered them again, shaking his head. "How can she not want our baby girl? She carried her, we felt her first kicks together, we both cried when we first held her ..."

Something broke in Mara as she heard Zane's voice catch. She leaned her head against the back of his shoulder, her hand sliding down his arm until she laced her fingers with his. He was almost cold to the touch, and she squeezed her eyes shut at the pain lancing through her in hearing this.

"How can she willingly give that up forever?" Zane asked hoarsely. "She's not an unfit mother, she's got the kind of life to support her. How can she look at our daughter and decide after all these years that she doesn't want her? I just ..." He shook his head before lowering it with a faint sniff. "Hope already doesn't remember much about her mom. I've tried, but I can't ... and now ... how do you tell a kid that one of their parents just flat out doesn't want them?"

Mara swallowed a wash of tears and softly kissed Zane's shoulder.

Zane sniffed again and sat up, prompting Mara to do the same. "I've talked with my lawyer a few times, and he's going to look into it. We'll give it to her, I guess, but we can't even do that yet. I haven't told my parents yet, I don't know how they'll respond. The Pit knows, and they're ready to start a war for Hope. That's something, I guess. I just ... I feel like I have failed Hope so spectacularly that it hurts to even look at her."

"How in the world have you failed Hope?" Mara demanded before she could stop herself. Rage roared through her veins, and she shoved at Zane's shoulder, forcing him to turn and face her. She took his face in hand and practically shook him. "It is *not* your fault that Michelle doesn't want to be a mother anymore. That's on her, not you. And if she feels this way, it's better that she's out now rather than when it might crush Hope. You are an incredible father, Zane, and your daughter adores you. She is so loved."

Her voice broke as she saw a tear leak from Zane's eye, and she wiped it away with her thumb. "So loved," she said again, her voice nearly as rough as his had been. "And she knows it. She's got you, your family, your friends, her classmates, me... my gosh, Zane, one of the things I love most about you is how you are with her. No father could love his daughter more than you do. If anything is your fault, it is that Hope is one of the greatest little girls I have ever met. Do not give that woman any more power in your life, or in Hope's. Don't."

Zane's eyes searched hers, hope and want and hurt giving their dark depths an earnest light that made Mara ache somewhere deep inside. He didn't say a word, he just reached out and ran his thumb along the side of Mara's face once, then again with a slow nod.

She'd take that as a response, and she leaned in for a hard kiss, not caring that he barely responded to it. "Okay. We need to do something tonight." She sniffed and stood, tugging him to a standing position. "My mom told me we need more cinnamon rolls. Let's go."

"Go?" he repeated as she pulled him down the path. "Go where?"

"The bakery," she called over her shoulder, her mind spinning as they walked, the bakery less than a block from where they were. "Kinda hard to make cinnamon rolls out here."

"You make them?"

Mara grinned and gave him a quick look. "Most of the time, yeah. Surprise."

There were no words for the delight that filled her at his laughing grin. Nobody knew that she was actually the mastermind behind their most popular pastry, and she liked to keep it that way. Her mom had put her own spin on the thing a time or two, but the family's classic cinnamon roll recipe was all Mara.

Now Zane would know it.

As he should.

Her parents greeted Zane with enthusiasm when they entered the kitchens, but also with a startling amount of normalcy, given that her mom immediately started directing Zane on where all necessary ingredients were. If they had thought anything of the pair of them holding hands when they arrived, they said nothing about it, much to Mara's relief. Zane took the apron from her dad with all good graces, and he even offered to sweep the floors once they were done, though neither of her parents would allow him to do that.

Once the pair were situated, her parents vanished with an airy, "Don't forget to lock up, Mars!"

Then there was silence.

Zane looked around the large kitchen, then at Mara with a surprised grin. "You planned this."

Mara held up her hands in surrender. "I did not, I will show you the text my mom sent me twenty minutes before we met up. I didn't even respond to it."

His eyes narrowed as though he didn't believe her. "Uh-huh. And your parents just happened to vacate the premises when we showed up?"

She could only shrug at that. "They are very smart people. And they like you."

Zane quirked his brows. "Not as much as their daughter, I'm guessing."

"I hope not," Mara shot back, propping a hand on her

hip. "That would be really awkward." She drummed her fingers on the countertop, then pointed at the large fridge behind him. "Open that up and get out a giant silver bowl."

He turned obediently and did as she asked while she sprinkled flour over the surface of the countertop before dusting her hands with flour. "Oh, and after you bring that here, why not turn on some music? System controls are over there in the corner."

"Any song requests, chef?" he inquired as he set the bowl down.

"Nothing that will make it feel like a rave is going on in here," she replied, unwrapping the bowl and pulling half of the dough out to set on the floured countertop.

She began patting the dough down when the strains of slow oldie songs reached her ears. She looked up at Zane in disbelief. "Really?"

He chuckled, shrugging as he came back over to her. "What can I say? I'm in the mood for slow songs with my girl and learning how she does all the incredible things she does."

A very slow, very hot wave began to cascade its way through her body, and she returned her attention to the dough, forcing a laugh as she pressed it out. "That's a list of maybe three things, and this is one of them. Lucky you."

"I was just thinking that. Lucky me."

The wave rolled again, and Mara exhaled through her nose, reaching for a nearby rolling pin and flouring the surface. "Ever attempted cinnamon rolls before?"

"Nope," Zane told her as he came over to her. "Mom went through a bread-making phase when I was ten or so, but that's about it. Tell me your secrets, goddess of mine."

Mara turned to face him, pointing the rolling pin at him. "Stop that. No flame-on, flame-off game with Mara while making baked goods, okay?"

"Flame on, flame off?" he repeated, grinning broadly. "That sounds like my kind of game, what are the rules?"

"No," Mara said in as firm a tone as she could manage while her legs shook. "Working here."

Zane nodded, wiping the grin from his face. "Understood. Tell me what you're doing."

She didn't trust his innocent expression, but this had all been her idea, so there was nothing else to do but get back to it. "Right. So I'm rolling this out into a big rectangle. Not too thin, but even."

"Looks good," he told her, nodding in approval as he took up position at her left shoulder. "Now what?"

What was it about him standing so close that immediately made her pulse race? She craned her neck and gestured to the butter that was sitting out, softening. "Stick that in the microwave, will you? Just needs to be melty."

Zane grunted. "Melty butter. Making things melt is my specialty."

Oh lands . . .

Mara took advantage of his back being turned to wipe at her brow, though she miraculously wasn't perspiring. "Oh good, should be a great job for you then," she managed to say without sounding breathless.

"Something in the oven?" Zane called as he fidgeted with the microwave. "Smells awesome."

"Mom whipped up a batch earlier," she told him. "I'll ice those when they're done."

He didn't need to know that, why had she told him that? Why was she rambling?

She fidgeted with the dough while Zane melted butter, the music somehow managing to build tension between them across the kitchen while they both wore stained aprons.

Great.

"Melty butter, as requested," Zane announced, somehow getting back to her without her hearing him.

"Great!" Her voice was too quick, but she covered by grabbing the bowl and gently pouring the butter along the surface of the dough. She grabbed a spoon and spread it around as evenly as possible. "Okay, can you hand me the blue bowl over there?"

It was in her hands in an instant. "Cinnamon sugar?" he guessed.

Mara smiled at that. "Yep. The recipe just says sugar. Trade secret: I use brown sugar. Much sweeter, brings the game to a whole new level."

"Does it?" Zane took a pinch of the mixture and dropped it into his mouth. "Wow. Yeah, much better."

"Zane," Mara scolded, rolling her eyes. "I need all of that for this batch. It's really specific." She started to sprinkle it over the buttered dough, ignoring how Zane was inching closer.

"A whole new level, you said," he murmured behind her. He reached for the bowl again, barely managing a pinch before Mara spun away, shaking her head at him, smiling in anticipation.

"Huh-uh. Let me finish."

He tilted his head at her. "Put the bowl down. Try this out."

"I've tried it," Mara assured him as she returned the bowl to the counter, warily watching him. "Lots of times."

"Come here," he coaxed, crooking a finger.

She shook her head again. "I don't think so."

His smile was slow and deliciously hot. "Flame on, Mara."

As if he truly had the power, her skin began to warm from her toes on upward, and though she didn't come closer, she didn't move away either. Zane came to her, his eyes trained on hers, the tension between them swirling almost painfully with every step. He stopped when he reached her, so close she could feel him when she breathed, and that awareness sent shocks skittering through her.

He raised his hand and sprinkled a pinch of cinnamon sugar along the crest of her cheeks, nose, and mouth, startling her. "What . . . ?"

His lips were on her skin before she could finish the question, and her breath snagged in her throat. His mouth dusted against the surface in faint brushes, lighting fires in their wake, and Mara's fingers flailed helplessly in response until they gripped his apron tightly. She arched her neck as he ran his lips down the column of her throat, though she couldn't recall if any speck of sugar had fallen there.

Zane's hands were at her hips, locking her in place, though there was no pressure there. The pressure was within her, building, burning, churning every sensation into something wild and desperate. She exhaled a shaky gasp of breath, which seemed to signal something to Zane, as he immediately raised his head and brought his mouth to hers, his kiss sharp and sure. The sweetness of the cinnamon sugar heightened everything, seared their connection into something forever imprinted on her heart, and Mara gave herself up to it. To him.

She tugged at him, raising herself up as she did so, crushing herself to him in a heady surrender that felt more like victory. His kiss turned deeper, slower, more filled with longing and adoration than anything Mara had imagined a kiss could be. She sighed into him, turning languid in his arms despite pressing herself into him. He hooked his fingers into the belt loops at her hips and hoisted her up into his arms, her legs wrapping around him as though they had been designed to do so.

He turned them slightly, just so she rested against the counter, and Mara folded her arms around his neck, her lips nipping at and molding with his in a slow, sensual dance. Again, Zane traced his lips along her throat, this time lingering where her shoulder started, dipping his lips into the hollow of her throat with a caress that elicited a mixture of a purr and growl from her. He chuckled against her skin and did it again, groaning when her legs tightened around him.

He nibbled his way back up to her chin, and Mara let him drag her mouth down to his for one more agonizing, painfully slow, impossibly thorough kiss.

Gradually, he pulled his mouth from hers, and dazedly, Mara opened her eyes, convinced she was seeing stars when she looked at him.

Zane didn't look quite that steady himself. He ran his hand over her hair, seeming to tremble slightly as he did so. "Brown-sugar-cinnamon-speckled Mara. Now that was delicious."

Mara let herself exhale very slowly, lowering her chin to give him a steady look. "You've ruined me for cinnamon rolls ever again," she rasped. "You know that, right?"

His grin clenched her stomach hard. "Sorry not sorry. Personally, I've always loved the taste of cinnamon rolls, but I definitely prefer the taste of you." He patted her hips and kissed her brow quickly. "Flame off, sweetheart, or we're never leaving. I'm gonna go stand over there and wait for the batch in the oven."

Mara nodded firmly. "Good idea." She unlocked her legs, which felt like Jell-O once they were freed, and watched Zane stride to the ovens, a much safer distance from her.

Lands. She needed to get this done and get out of this overheated kitchen before something else overheated entirely.

But not before she got in one final jab. "Hey, babe?"

Zane froze at the oven and, almost warily, looked over his shoulder at her.

Mara lifted her shoulder in a half shrug where she sat. "You're not so bad sweetened up yourself."

His gaze darkened, and he shook his head. "You don't play fair, Mara."

"Rule number one of this game, Zane," she said with a slow smile. "Fair play is highly overrated."

"What's rule number two?" he asked with a laugh.

She hopped down off of the counter, her legs still shaking slightly. "I'll tell you in Chicago this weekend."

A wild grin exploded across his face, nearly making Mara cry or laugh or some combination of the two. "You're coming with me?"

"Yeah," she replied around the lump in her throat. "Yeah, baby, I'm coming with you."

# FIFTEEN

"It's fine. It's absolutely fine, no pressure, no worries. It's fine."

"What are you whining about?"

Zane looked at Rocco darkly. "Rock, I don't like speeches."

Rocco rolled his eyes without any sympathy. "You lost, you get to make the speech. Just say, 'Thanks for coming, thanks for your support, we hope this new team room brings the spirit of Northbrook back into the teams that come through here,' then say something nice about Coach, and cut the stupid ribbon."

Zane raised a brow and turned to Trane in the limo. "You got a notepad or something? I want to get that down before I forget it."

Trane grunted a laugh and smacked his hand away. "Just pretend it's reporters instead of suits. Besides, we only have to stay an hour, then we're off to birthday festivities, right?" He looked around the limo at the rest of them. "Right?"

They whooped, and Zane shook his head, chuckling to himself. "What did you guys have in mind? And by the way, Hope is so excited."

"Hope's excited?" Jax barked a laugh. "Dice can't stop giggling, he's so jazzed. It's like the guy never had a birthday party."

Laughter filled the limo while Declan protested, and Zane felt himself relaxing slightly. He really did hate making speeches, always had. He could play hockey in front of thousands, could take postgame interviews without breaking a sweat, but put him at a press conference or in a suit at a podium and he forgot what words were.

Since he'd lost at their late-night card game last night, Zane had been named their spokesman of the day, which the others were delighted about, and he would have paid any of them some decent money to do for him.

Unfortunately, they all made just as much as he did, if not more, so they weren't tempted by his numbers.

He'd been trying all morning.

He was actually getting ready to up the ante, come to think.

"Are we there yet?" Rocco asked loudly, looking out the window.

Being with these guys was ridiculous, without fail, but it was also a riot. He'd gotten in yesterday with Hope, while Mara was flying in this morning, and his daughter hadn't stopped smiling since. The guys had insisted she come to dinner last night, and they'd all somehow managed to talk Trane into splitting a dessert with her.

She'd come over to the facility with Mara a little later, but he wished they were with him now.

He'd feel much more comfortable about a stupid speech with them there. Mara had a way of calming him down with just a smile or a look, and everything about Hope made him happier.

Coach Fenwick was being honored at this event. Coach

Fenwick, who had taken the time to talk Zane through his fears of his parents' divorce. Coach Fenwick, who had never once made a comment about Zane's size, good or bad, when it came to playing hockey. Coach Fenwick, who had found that extra gear in Zane's athleticism that he hadn't known he had.

He had to make a speech honoring that man and dedicating the new team room named for him.

No pressure or anything.

He exhaled slowly as they pulled up to the Northbrook facilities, and Zane frowned as he looked out of the window.

"Huh. It looks like nothing has changed."

For a beat, no one said a thing.

"Come on," Clint insisted. "The landscaping is totally improved."

"The birds' nests are gone," Declan remarked with a nod as he eyed the letters on the building.

"Get out," Jax insisted, pushing Rocco towards the door of the limo.

A scuffle worthy of a group of nine-year-olds ensued as the six of them fought for the position of first to exit, and Trane won the spot, being the largest and toughest. Thankfully, the press weren't waiting for them, so no one cared about their arrival.

Once they entered the building, however, things were different.

The six of them were immediately ushered up to the new team room, where Bree Stone and her small but mighty band of cohorts took charge. Bree might be Clint's girlfriend, and one of Zane's favorite people, but she didn't mess around, and Darci, her PR associate, directed them all with a brisk efficiency that left no room for argument or question.

Not that Zane would have argued or questioned. He'd

love to have all of this over sooner rather than later, and if anyone could make that happen for him, he'd do whatever was asked.

Darci and Bree were so efficient, as it happened, that the guys were set before anyone else was.

Bree smiled at them all, shrugging. "Well, go ahead and have a look around, I guess. We've got a few minutes before we get going." She gave Zane a look. "You did arrange for the little bug to come to this, right?"

Zane threw his hands up in mock disgruntlement. "Does everybody want her to be here more than me?"

"Yes," at least four people said without missing a beat.

Zane shook his head, then looked at Bree with a smile. "Yes, she'll be here. Mara's bringing her."

Bree's eyes brightened, her smile turning wry. "Mara, huh? Can't wait to meet her." She turned and slipped her arm around Clint's waist, walking away with him, Clint kissing the side of her head as they stole a moment.

The action caught Zane in the center of his chest, somehow connecting with nerves in his left foot. He wanted that with Mara, wanted the easy comfort of being together no matter who was around. The natural draw towards each other, a gravitational pull filled with energy and tension, the warmth that came with breathing the same air and inhabiting the same space.

They fit; that was the sense filling him at this moment. Clint and Bree just fit.

Mara could be his perfect fit.

He prayed like hell he could be hers.

"Z! Get a load of this!" Jax called with a laugh.

Zane shook himself out of his mooning stupor and ambled over to one of the photo murals on the wall. He chuckled almost immediately upon seeing it.

He and Jax were maybe fourteen and roughly the same size, though Jax outweighed him by at least fifteen pounds, and their elite squad teammates were lined up with them. It was one of the intersquad games, so the other guys weren't pictured, being the opposing line, but somehow it still managed to capture their energy and attitude.

If punk fourteen-year-olds trying to look intimidating could have energy and attitude.

Zane swore softly as his eyes traced over the faces of other guys they had once played with, guys he hadn't thought of in years. "That feels like a lifetime ago, but I'm pretty sure I could recall every minute of that game."

"Same here." Jax tapped the image of one of the guys in their lineup. "Ryan Waters. Remember him? He was supposed to be better than all of us put together."

"Jeez, I haven't heard that name in a long time," Declan commented as he came over. "How long has it been?"

"Ten years," Zane murmured, remembering all too clearly the day Coach Fenwick had come to practice with tears in his eyes to tell them Ryan had been killed in a car accident. They'd all worn the number seventeen for him in the next home game, and it had gone down in Northbrook history as the greatest game they'd ever played. It had also been the first game where Zane had collected more than one penalty and learned the value of working the crowd.

Ryan would have loved that.

A somber silence fell over them all as they stared at his picture together.

"Hey, there's my princess!"

Zane blinked at Jax's exclamation, turning to see who he meant. To no one's surprise, Hope stood there in a bright-green dress, her hand tucked in that of a gorgeous woman in a long navy dress, belted at the waist, which gave her already perfect body some serious oomph. He couldn't even see her legs, and his throat was going dry.

Mara fidgeted with the scarf draped around her neck, her smile wavering as she glanced around the room.

"Uncle Jax!" Hope squealed, releasing Mara's hand as she ran to Jax.

He swooped her up and swung her around, then held her at his chest, giving her a serious look. "Now, who did you come here with, bug? I don't know her."

"That's Miss Mara," Hope said at once, beaming a grin at her. "She's my dance teacher, and I think she's Daddy's girlfriend."

All of the guys snickered at that, and Zane shook his head with a sigh.

Better make his mark, then.

He strode over to Mara with a warm smile. "Hey, you."

Her relieved smile back at him was everything. "Hey, you."

He leaned down to kiss her cheek, slipping his arm possessively around her, tugging her close to his side. "You okay?"

She nodded, her blue eyes bluer than he could ever remember seeing. "Much better now that you're here."

"Mara," Jax said then, sticking his hand out with a grin. "Nice to see your face in person."

Zane glowered, but Mara only shook Jax's hand, her mouth curving in a playful smile. "Jax. I was told you're not my type."

One of the guys choked on a laugh, but Jax's eyes only narrowed at them both. "Really? And?"

Mara didn't respond right away, but she shook his hand once more. "He was right."

"Shots fired!" Rocco bellowed while Declan and Trane only laughed in near hysterics.

Zane kissed Mara's cheek again, sliding his lips to her ear. "That's my girl."

She slapped his back, her cheeks turning pink but her smile tempting him to say more.

So much more.

"Okay, guys," Bree announced as she reentered the room with Clint, Coach Fenwick behind them. "Ready?" She stopped at seeing Mara, then grinned. "You've got to be Mara."

Mara's smile turned hesitant again. "Guilty."

"You're coming with me." Bree looped her arm through Mara's, pulling her from Zane. "Come on, bug, we're going over here, okay?"

"Okeydoke." Hope nearly hopped out of Jax's arms and took Bree's free hand as she led them over to the other side of the room.

"Yeesh," Zane muttered, watching as Bree chatted with Mara out of his earshot. "That makes me nervous."

"I beg your pardon?" Clint laughed and clapped him on the shoulder. "My girlfriend is not that nosey."

Zane gave him a sidelong look. "And mine isn't that open."

Clint shrugged. "No worries then." He pushed Zane forward, towards the reporters now filtering into the room.

Showtime.

Zane forced a smile, shook Coach Fenwick's hand, and nodded at whatever his coach said, though he didn't actually take any of it in. He was too busy fighting the urge to check the position of his hair, the band in it suddenly feeling like a snake strangling the life out of him.

He turned to the reporters and cleared his throat. "Good morning," he announced as he folded his hands loosely before him. "Thank you for coming today."

The reporters all kind of nodded, turning on their phones or mics, photographers snapping a few pics early.

"The six of us," Zane went on, gesturing to their group, "and every other proud Sabercat that has ever sat in this room before, are thrilled to have the support of the community and our new sponsors to make this renovation possible. It seems only right to dedicate this new team room to the man who has dedicated his life and his career to furthering the development of hockey players here at Northbrook."

Zane paused and turned to smile at Coach, standing next to him with an almost sheepish expression. "Coach Fenwick and his impact on Northbrook Hockey are legendary, and there is no one who deserves this honor more than him. It is our hope that in his name, in his honor, every future Sabercat entering this room will feel the pride, the power, and the privilege that it is to be among us, and they will know that they carry with them the support of us all. Thank you very much."

Applause filled the room and Zane stepped forward to shake Coach Fenwick's hand, smiling in surprise when Coach pulled him in for a quick hug.

"Thanks, Z," the older man grunted. "Thanks for being here."

Zane patted his back. "Wouldn't miss it, Coach. You deserve this."

Darci stepped forward with a pair of shears and directed Zane to one of the doors, where a green-and-white-striped ribbon was tied. Biting back a sigh, Zane posed with the club president, Mr. White, and Coach Fenwick for a few pictures, then snipped the ribbon to the general applause of reporters, sponsors, and whoever else had showed up. He handed the shears to Darci with a nod, waved to the cameras, then turned back to the guys.

"So moving," Trane muttered through a smile. "Really."

"They'll be making motivational videos from that any minute," Rocco added.

"Shut up," Zane snapped before turning around, clapping his hands on the shoulders of them both for a few more photos.

"Three on three after this?" Clint asked, somehow without moving his lips.

"Nah. I got my girls here." Zane glanced over at them both, winking.

His daughter stood in front of Mara, whose arms were draped over her shoulders and holding her hands, swinging them back and forth in the air. She grinned at Zane and looked up at Mara, pointing at him. He saw Mara's smile spread and felt his own smile do the same.

It was an automatic response. Mara just made him smile.

"Right, we done?" Zane said suddenly, returning his attention to the photographers. Without waiting for a response, he looked over at Bree. "Bree, we good?"

Bree gave him a thumbs-up, grinning knowingly. "Good, thanks, guys."

Zane nodded and moved away from the guys to scoop up Hope and take Mara's hand. "Come on. We'll take a quick tour of the place, and then ... it's somebody's birthday, so we've got some celebrating to do!"

Hope gasped and took Zane's face in her hands. "Really, Daddy? Can we?"

"Yesh," he said though squished cheeks. "I fink so, but I can't feew my faesh."

Hope giggled and released his face. "You're a dork, Daddy."

"I know." Zane grinned and turned her to face the guys. "We ready, boys?"

Declan whooped and came over with a clap of his hands,

opening his arms. "Uncle Dice wants to be your tour guide, Hope. You good with that?"

"Yay!" Hope cheered and extended her arms towards him, making Declan laugh as he took her from Zane's hold. "Let's go!"

Never one to bypass an opportunity, Declan immediately turned and strode for the door, tickling Hope as he went, the other guys following them.

"Wow," Mara murmured, her fingers rubbing across his in their hold. "They really do love her."

Zane snorted softly. "Yeah. And they won't waste a moment turning her against me, so let's catch up." He started for the door, tugging Mara behind him, her snickers making him laugh as well.

Their group wandered around the entire facility, with Bree joining them about halfway through. Hope laughed the entire time, thanks to the stories, antics, and commentary from her uncles, so he didn't have to worry about her for a second, leaving him to focus more on Mara. She was quiet but stayed close to him, smiling and letting him tell her anything and everything about Northbrook. She took it all in, asking only a few questions, but aside from her hand constantly being in his, he wouldn't have known she was there had he not seen her.

"You okay there?" Zane asked finally as they headed to the car after the impromptu tour finished. "You're not saying much."

Mara smiled up at him and pulled his own move on him, brushing a stray lock of hair out of his face and stroking his cheek in the process. "I'm fantastic," she assured him as she sent a jolt of sensation up his spine. "I feel like I just watched home videos from your childhood, and I find you absolutely adorable."

He chuckled and tugged her closer, leaning down to brush his nose against hers. "How adorable?"

She pressed up to her toes and kissed him softly. "Very."

"Hey, lovebirds, let's go!" Rocco bellowed. "Hope picked a birthday venue, and we gotta change!"

"Change?" Zane repeated, frowning at his friend as he stood by the cars. "For what?"

"The arcade, Daddy!" Hope beamed at him from the limo. "Uncle Jax says it's the best!"

Zane groaned under his breath, shaking his head. "Well, if Uncle *Jax* says so . . ."

Mara nudged him, laughing. "Stop. It'll be fun. Look how happy she is."

He could see how happy his daughter was and knew how much fun something like this could be for her. Truth be told, he was touched. It was one thing for him and Mara to give up their night in the city for Hope's birthday, but these five guys, and Bree, were willing to do the same. Not many people would choose to spend their time with a newly minted six-year-old girl, but they were.

It was incredible, and as Hope's father, he was touched.

"Let's go, babe," he murmured to Mara. "This could be gold."

Only an hour later, their group pulled up to a Jax-approved location, and Zane burst into laughter at seeing it.

"What?" Mara asked as the others joined in.

"Rally-Kats was the token location for all of our team celebrations when the season ended," Zane explained. He climbed out of the car and offered her a hand, pulling her flush against his side and draping an arm around her shoulders as they headed for the entrance, Hope riding in style on top of Trane's shoulders.

Mara looked at the building in surprise. "This place? Really?"

"Oh yeah," Clint told her as he came alongside her, Bree's hand in his. "Pizza parties were nothing unless they happened here." He laughed at Mara's dubious expression. "I promise, they've updated the place since we were here last."

"Who cares?" Jax turned around to walk backwards, grinning at Mara. "I bet I can beat you in Pac-Man, Mara Matthews."

A burst of pride lit up Zane's chest as Mara's brows snapped down at the bet. "You're on, Jax. I own you."

"Kick his trash, babe," Zane whispered against her ear before kissing her cheek.

"Zamboni style," she confirmed with a nod.

It was a glorious thing to behold, once they got inside, had their table set, and were each in possession of handfuls of tokens. Mara's more competitive side—which, as it happened, rivaled any of the hockey players'—led to a Pac-Man tournament with most of the guys, which she won in the end. Hope had somehow managed to secure a tiara for herself and rotated among various games and activities.

Rally-Kats was the perfect place for her. Lit by the gaming screens, blacklights, and a ceiling strewn with strings of neon lights that winked brighter in a pattern set to the music pumping through the speakers, it was both mysterious and magical. The place was fairly crowded, but there were enough gaming stations for all, including some very Hope-geared, sparkle-encased ones that scared him beyond belief.

"Dance-off!" His daughter squealed when she caught sight of it, twirling in her white and pink tutu skirt she had specifically picked out for her birthday. "Mara! Mara, Mara, can we do it?"

Mara laughed, tucking her long T-shirt into the back of her jeans. "Sure, sweetie. Let's hit it!" She held her hand out, and Hope snatched it at once, racing off towards the glittering disco floor of the machine.

Zane watched them do the steps of the dances, leaning against a pinball machine and grinning without reserve. It was hard to tell who was having more fun; Mara seemed to laugh just as much as Hope, and both of them were reaching successive levels with their scores.

This was what every birthday should be like for his daughter. Full of laughter and fun, not disappointing voicemails and changing plans.

"I like her."

Zane turned to see Bree coming up beside him. "Who, Hope? Yeah, she's great."

Bree gave him a look, shaking her head. "Mara."

"I know." He smiled and returned his attention to the dancing. "She's incredible. Real. Perfect, even."

"No one's perfect, Zane," Bree reminded him gently.

He nodded but didn't say anything. He knew that; he had proof of that. His once-perfect woman had turned into a heartbreaking nightmare, and it had taken him this long to recover enough to try a serious relationship again. But what he felt for Mara was so much more than anything he'd had with Michelle. Mara wasn't perfect; what he felt for Mara was perfect.

What they had together was perfect.

And that was terrifying. Exhilarating, but terrifying.

Straightening, Zane exhaled and turned to Bree. "Whac-A-Mole, Bree?"

She obliged him, losing with good graces, only to then crush him at Skee-Ball in retaliation. Rocco spent his time racking up points in the racing game while Declan focused on his target shooting, both of them collecting dozens of tickets, making every ten-year-old in the place insanely jealous.

It was just as hard to pull them away from their games as it was to get Hope away, even for something as delicious and motivating as pizza could be. The dining area was slightly better lit than the arcade area, and somehow they managed to squeeze their entire group into a corner booth. Presents for Hope were produced, some even wrapped, and Zane shook his head at the expense of some of them.

"Oh, come on, man!" he protested when Hope opened a full makeup kit from Rocco that made the birthday girl scream with glee. "Seriously?"

"Not your birthday, *Dad*." Rocco gave him a superior look as Hope smothered him with hugs and kisses. "It's from Summer, too. She says hi."

"That's worse than the karaoke machine! Which, by the way, I'm also not okay with." He glared at Clint at this.

Clint was also unimpressed. "Don't be a killjoy." He slid a plate with a large slice of pepperoni pizza over to him. "Shut up and eat your pizza."

"That's not a nice word, Uncle Clint," Hope announced, her expression turning disapproving.

The guys ate that up, and Declan leaned closer to Hope. "What's the punishment for that, princess? You decide."

Hope looked at Clint through narrowed eyes, and Zane decided he had never been more proud of his daughter in his entire life than at that moment.

She stunned the table by plucking her tiara from her head and passing it across the table. "Wear my tiara and sing 'Happy Birthday' to me by yourself."

Scratch that. *Now* he had never been more proud of his daughter.

The table erupted with cheers and laughter, egging Clint on with great enthusiasm. He was a good sport, put on the tiara, and, after a fantastic drumroll from the group, did the job well. Then he followed it up by challenging every guy at the table to a match at the air hockey table he had seen to one side of the arcade games, shockingly free of users at the moment.

Even Hope had cheered at that, once she'd reclaimed her tiara, and their booth cleared, pizza remains abandoned, for the sake of the new challenge.

Clint and Declan were up first; their trash talk attracted a few spectators, if their competitive natures didn't. Zane led the charge in taunting both of them, keeping his language and his tone tamer than he would have on the ice, given their location and the age of the birthday girl vying for the best vantage point for the game. Their excitement didn't seem to match their surroundings, but none of them seemed to care about that.

Hockey was hockey, and they gave it their all.

The game ended in a shootout, and each of them gave Hope a turn to take the shot, letting her score each time, to her delight.

Rocco and Jax were the next game, and their energy drew an actual crowd, which was no surprise. Jax was the hometown hero, despite the entire gang being from Chicago, and it didn't take long for people to realize he was with his friends. Sides were chosen among the onlookers, and Zane shook his head with a laugh as he saw money being exchanged by a few.

Someone brushed against him, and Zane turned, surprised that Mara was edging closer, her attention not on the game. "Zane..."

"What?" He followed her gaze and saw some teens recording the game on their phones and at least three others typing away on theirs, clearly invested in the game as well as their messages.

Strange, what was so exciting about grown men getting into air hockey?

"It's Jax," Zane assured her gently, pulling her into his side. "He's a big deal here. It's okay."

Mara didn't look convinced, and to be honest, Zane wasn't that convinced either.

The further the game went, the more the crowd grew. Chants for Rocco were heard, but more people were there for Jax. There were full-on cheers with every goal and block, enough that even Zane was getting jostled by onlookers wanting to see.

He frowned, biting the inside of his cheek. Then he nudged the guy next to him, one of the phone-typers. "What's going on?"

"Dude, it's Jax and his Northbrook gang," came the excited reply. "They were in town for this thing, it was on the news, and now they're here just playing around. It's some girl's birthday, someone said, and it's all over Twitter, look." He showed Zane his phone, where several tweets with the hashtag *#NorthbrookChallenge* were scrolling.

Zane's stomach dropped. The challenge had been one of their earliest attempts at bringing attention to the club a few months ago, but it had taken the sports world by storm. It had only recently stopped trending, as the videos of new challenges had dropped off significantly.

Now it was back, given that these Northbrook guys were challenging each other. And the crowd was growing.

The guy finally looked up at him, and his eyes widened. "Dude! You're . . . you're Zamboni! Holy crap, can I get a selfie?"

"Daddy?" Hope's scared voice broke through the noise, and there was a beat of near silence in the crowd at hearing it.

Zane looked at his daughter, fear and realization hitting at the same time.

"Happy birthday!" someone from the crowd called,

noting Hope's tiara and proximity to the table, or perhaps that her hand was in Trane's. Whatever it was, it sent the rest of the crowd reaching for their phones, the ones already out snapping photos.

Something in Zane snapped, and he turned to the nearest phone pointing at his daughter, snatching it from the hands of its owner and chucking it across the room.

Chaos erupted, and a few faces of reporters Zane had seen at their event earlier were now seen in the crowd, inching their way towards the air hockey table and Hope.

"Jax!" Zane bellowed as he dodged a blow from his robbery victim.

Jax met his eyes at once, the same fury evident in his face, and he nodded without question. He picked up Hope and, using Trane as a bouncer, shield, and battering ram, forced his way through the crowd. Zane took an elbow to the stomach then, and he wheezed painfully before turning to slam the guy into the gate-like railing nearby.

The crash of breaking glass could be heard, and over the din, a few employees tried to call out instructions to the fighters that were ignored.

"Zane!"

He whirled at Mara's cry, wincing as he caught someone else's blow across his cheek. Mara was getting pushed back towards the dining area amid the chaos, and her fear was evident. He shook his head, charging through the people and shoving some aside to get to her.

"You're bleeding!" Mara gasped when he reached her, touching his now-tender cheek.

"Whatever. Come on." He took her hand, tucking her behind him as he tried to move them towards the door.

"Running from a fight, Zamboni?" someone taunted from the crowd. "Some party."

"Who's the girl, Z?" another called.

A roaring sound answered both, and Zane almost swore as he saw Trane all out punch someone in the face, a phone flying in the direction of the arcade windows seconds after. Then an expensive-looking camera crashed to the floor, and sirens could be heard.

Now Zane *did* swear. He looked around, Mara's hand still in his, and found Clint reaching them, Bree close behind. "We gotta get out of here," he told Clint. "Or at least get the girls out. I'll handle the cops, pay for any damages."

Clint shook his head, a hand going to Zane's shoulder. "Don't worry about that. We're good, Rocco's gonna handle the cops, and Diesel and Dice have cleanup. Let's go."

Zane nodded, his concern for his daughter outweighing any sense of guilt for leaving. The four of them headed out to the parking lot and were in their cars driving away before anyone said anything else.

The car was silent on the drive to the hotel. It was all Zane could do not to floor it and ignore all speed limits and traffic signals. If he had been by himself, he would have done it, but with a shaken Mara with him . . .

"Is it always like that?" Mara whispered.

Zane shook his head. "No. But . . ." He exhaled roughly. "If any of our teams get hot, go to the playoffs, if we're in the wrong crowd . . . and with us hyping ourselves out for Northbrook . . ."

"So it could get like that, is what you're saying."

"Not like *that*," he assured her, jerking his thumb towards the arcade. "That was a mob."

Mara didn't seem to hear him, her eyes focused straight ahead.

He didn't like her blank expression, the complete lack of emotion, or the fact that he had no idea what she was thinking when he had been able to tell so well only an hour ago.

"Mara."

"Let's just check on Hope," she murmured without looking at him. "It's going to be a late night."

There was no telling what she could mean by that, and quite frankly, Zane was afraid to ask. She didn't sound like herself, and he couldn't say he blamed her. A brawl on the ice was one thing, but a brawl in real life? At a birthday party?

Zane didn't have it in him to respond, but his grip on the steering wheel tightened.

He wasn't sure how much time had passed since he'd seen Jax leave with Hope, or what time that had been, but the need to hold his daughter had never been this powerful in his life. Her terrified cry would haunt him tonight, and possibly every other night for the foreseeable future.

His phone buzzed, and his attention went to it where it sat in the cupholder. He sighed heavily at the message. "Hope's with Jax in his room watching a movie. He says she's okay."

Mara's head turned as she looked out of her window. "Good."

The hotel was before them soon enough, and Zane strode into it with long strides, Mara right behind him. The elevator ride was as silent as the car had been, and as they walked down the hall to Jax's room, the strangest sense of unease filled him. Not danger, but something that made him feel like he was coiling up or bracing for impact.

He knocked on Jax's door when they reached it, and Jax was quick to open up and let them in, his finger at his lips. "She just passed out on the bed. Total sugar coma, didn't even make it halfway through the movie."

Zane nodded and crept towards the bedroom portion of the suite. Tiara still on her head, Hope lay curled on the bed, clutching a huge purple teddy bear, whatever fear she'd felt earlier completely gone.

"Where'd that thing come from?" Zane asked, turning to raise a brow at Jax.

"What do you think we did with all of our tickets?" His friend grinned, shoving his hands into his pockets and shrugging. "It's her birthday, man."

The events of the night suddenly caught up with him, and Zane sank onto the couch nearby, rubbing his hands over his face. "Thanks for getting her out of there, J," he rasped, looking over at Jax. "I couldn't have gotten to her that fast, and..."

"Stop," Jax interrupted with a shake of his head. "If you think there's a guy among us who would do anything less, you're crazy."

Zane nodded, swallowing hard. "How bad is it going to be?" he asked in a low voice.

"Diesel just called, it's already wrapped up." Jax sat next to him on the couch, rubbing his hands together. "Cops understand, they're making some inquiries, but we're all in the clear. Rally-Kats isn't going to press charges. Social media is blowing up, though."

"I was afraid of that." Zane pinched the bridge of his nose and sighed. "What are they saying?"

"Lots of speculation about who said 'Daddy' in all of that mess, and whose party it was." Jax hissed slowly, shaking his head. "Rumors flying that she's Diesel's kid, actually."

"Great. It'll make the rounds for all of us. I'm sorry, J, I'll put out a statement, clear you guys from the gossip..."

Jax gripped his shoulder hard, silencing him. "Did you hear me, Zane? All of us would have gotten Hope out of there or taken on the whole room. None of us care about people thinking Hope is ours. We'd all claim her if we had to, and we're all going to protect her. Don't say another word about it. Okay?"

There were no words for that, and Zane just lowered his head, the weight of his emotions almost overpowering him. Jax gave his shoulder another squeeze before rising from the couch and stepping away into another room of the suite, quietly answering a call.

"Zane?"

Mara's soft voice raised his head. "Yeah, babe?"

Her smile was soft, tired, and almost sad. "I'm gonna go."

He nodded, sniffing once. "Yeah, it's pretty late. You need to get some sleep." He stood up with a sigh.

Mara shook her head, stopping him, her throat working on a swallow. "No, Zane. I'm gonna go. Back home. Tonight."

He blinked. "What? Baby, you can't, it's late, and you just got here. We've got another day tomorrow, and tonight . . ." He took a step towards her, hand outstretched. "Tonight wasn't . . ."

"It's not about tonight," she interrupted gently, holding up a restraining hand and staying where she was. "It's about us."

Zane's entire body froze, and his breath seized up. "What's wrong with us?"

Mara's eyes shone with tears that almost buckled his knees. "Nothing. Nothing is wrong with us. We are amazing. We are intense and deep, and this whole thing is so much more than I ever thought it would be."

He stared at her, barely moving. "It scares you."

"To death," she said with a nod. "Zane . . . I love you."

Three little words. Just three words, and ones that should have lit into him like fire but instead sunk a weight into his stomach, anchoring him to the floor. "Mara . . ."

"I love you," she repeated, the words faster this time. "And it is so fast for me to say that. Doesn't make it less true or less real, it's just a lot. All of this is a lot. And I need to be sure." She swallowed again, her eyes somehow steady on his even though he could see her shaking. "You deserve to have me be sure."

"I'm sure," he managed, his throat aching with the words. "I love you. I love you so much, Mara, and this is it."

"I hope so." She smiled at him, but the smile made something in his heart crack. "I really hope so. I want this to be it. But that game the other night, and being here with you, and celebrating with Hope . . ." She shook her head, wetting her lips. "Honey, you need me to be sure. To be all in. Hope deserves someone in her life that is sure she's all in. I can't take a chance on that. And you don't want me to."

Agony began to wring his entire frame like a rag, and his chest tightened with it. "Mara, please . . ."

She sniffled and took a step back. "I'm not leaving you. I just need time. It would be best if you don't message me for a bit."

"Don't cut me out of your life." He shook his head, his eyes burning in synchrony with his throat. "Please . . ."

"I'm practically addicted to you, Zane," Mara admitted. "It will be so easy to just give in to you if we stay in touch."

"And that's a bad thing?" This couldn't be happening, not here, not now, not with them . . .

Mara exhaled slowly, her lips curving into a tender smile that would surely kill him. "You deserve more than that. And so does the sweet girl in that room. If this is it, Zane, it will happen. I'm not giving up. I'm just making sure."

"Then why does it feel like goodbye?" he demanded softly, his voice breaking at last.

She didn't answer that; she only bit her lip and turned for the door.

"How long do you need?" he asked, unable to help himself.

Mara looked over her shoulder at him, one hand on the door. "I don't know," she admitted. "But I hope not long." She smiled again, then left the room, the click of the closing door sounding more like the clanging of a jail cell.

And just as ominous.

# SIXTEEN

"Finish up strong, kids! Here we go. Five, six, seven, eight, jump!"

Mara bit back a laugh even as she jumped from side to side with the kids, watching as half of them were offbeat but their energy was high. They had all been great today, doing everything she had asked without whining or complaint, and some of the routines they had been working on were coming much easier to them now. They were following along without as much trouble, and some of the kids who had been struggling most were actually getting things now.

It was one of the days where she was glad she was doing this; not just for the kids but for herself.

She had accomplished something with this class, which was more than she could say for anything else lately.

One week since she had seen Zane. Or talked to him. Or texted him.

One minute since she had thought of him, but one week since she'd had any connection with him.

One week felt like one year.

She stood by her decision to take a breather, but it had

been agony. After the intensity of their almost constant communication and spending every available moment together, the expanse of nothing was just acutely painful. It had taken regular reminders to herself that this had been her call, that she hadn't been abandoned, and that she needed to use this time wisely.

The amount of tears she had cried might not have been wise, but they had given her more to consider.

She loved Zane, wildly and deeply. She wanted nothing more than to drop everything and rush over to his house just to be in his arms for one minute more.

The yearning for him hadn't subsided during the week; it had only intensified. Settled in. Taken root.

She couldn't have claimed a honeymoon phase when she had cut off all contact with him. She couldn't have claimed he'd swayed her, charmed her into staying, or that she hadn't had her eyes open. They were wide open, and what she was seeing was devastating.

This wasn't a whirlwind she had been caught up in; this was real.

Really real.

She smiled as she remembered Zane saying the same thing to her only a few weeks ago, when all this had started. It had felt real to her then, but it was nothing compared to how she felt now.

Time away from Zane had made her want him all the more.

And that was real too.

"And now the big finish!" she called out to her class. They marched in place forward and backwards with her, then jumped to the left, the right, and clapped their way up to the front of the room where she was, punching the air as the song ended.

"Woohoo!" Mara cheered and grinned down at them all. "That was the best one yet! Give yourselves a hand!"

The kids clapped and cheered, a few giggling as they did so.

Mara heaved a sigh, wiping her brow. "Okay, that's all for today. Get your stuff and go see Miss Hannah. We'll see you next week."

They trickled away in small groups, spreading out to grab their things from the edges of the room, and started to file out towards the desk.

"Miss Mara!"

A lump formed in Mara's throat in an instant as a small body slammed itself against her, tiny arms wrapping around her waist in a tight embrace. Tears welled as Mara instinctively reached down to return the hug, and she sniffed them back, blinking hard. "Hi, pumpkin. How are you?"

"So good," Hope replied, pulling back to look up at her. "My grandmas gave me the stuffed animal I wanted from the store in the mall! We went to build it right after my birthday party at Grandma Rae's house."

Mara sank to the floor, smiling warmly and taking Hope's hand in hers. "That sounds awesome! Did you have a fun birthday party with your family?"

Hope nodded eagerly, her pigtails bouncing with the motion. "Papa Tom let me drive his truck around the neighborhood with him, and Aunt Julie made a ginormous cake. It had like three levels, Miss Mara, and it was all pink!"

"Was it yummy?" Mara asked, throat tightening with emotion and a wistful wish that she had stayed for that party, if for no other reason than to see Hope experience it.

"Delicious," Hope gushed. "I had so many presents that Daddy had to put them in a box to mail to us. He said I was not getting any presents next year because I had so many this year." She rolled her eyes, then giggled. "He's so silly like that."

The mention of Zane caught Mara in the chest, and for a moment, breathing and swallowing were impossible. "It sounds like you had the bestest party ever, sweetheart. I'm sorry I missed it."

Hope grinned at her and gave her another hug. "That's okay. Daddy said you had to go home. Did you have a good time?"

The sweetness of the question almost brought Mara to tears again, and the fact that there was no other question, no resentment, no *my daddy misses you* added to it made everything more perfect.

Mara held the precious girl tightly for a moment, swallowing hard. "Not as good as your party would have been, but that's okay. Thank you for asking."

"Daddy says it's supposed to get warm next week," Hope stated as she pulled back again. "Maybe we can go to the park. Want to go with us?"

"I would love to," Mara told her, rubbing her arms. "We'll see what our schedule looks like, okay?"

Hope nodded before dashing over to pick up her coat. "Bye, Miss Mara. I'm gonna go get pancakes with Daddy now!"

It was on the tip of her tongue to ask to come with, but she clamped her teeth down to stop herself and only waved. She watched Hope dash out of the room and was unable to stop herself from following, her pace much slower than the girl's rapid-fire one.

The large windows of the gym were both a blessing and a curse as Mara made her way through the machines, following Josie and Hope at a far enough distance to not be seen. She barely saw them, her attention focused on the parking lot through the tinted windows, eyes scanning for the tall form she loved most in the world.

Her breath caught as she saw him on the sidewalk waiting, baseball cap on his head, hands in the pockets of his coat, his eyes on the building. He wouldn't be able to see her, thanks to the protective tinting of the windows, but nothing obstructed her view of him. He was more gorgeous than she had ever seen him, and far and away more casually dressed than she had ever seen him. His expression was unreadable, but he looked tired somehow, his eyes almost lazily tracing over the facade of the gym as a whole.

They stopped on the windows, and for a breathless heartbeat, Mara thought he could see her. Then his gaze dropped lower, staring at nothing. She watched as his Adam's apple bobbed, and her heart did a similar motion in response.

He was looking for her.

There was no reason she should suspect that, and no way she could know for sure, but her heart wouldn't listen to logic. Zane was looking for her. Was missing her. Wanted her.

This past week had almost killed her, but what had it done to him? Had he understood what she had been saying? Would he hate her for leaving like that? Did he believe that she loved him?

*I love you so much, Mara, and this is it.*

His words echoed in her mind, and she grasped onto them tightly. She had to believe that still held; she *had* to.

Holding Hope in her arms had felt like breathing fresh air, and seeing Zane now, knowing he couldn't see her, might as well have been sinking into a warm bath at the end of a long day. It settled the decision in her mind and heart in an instant, with more clarity than the last week had brought her, even after hours and hours of endless debates with herself.

They were her home. And she desperately wanted to come home.

Mara stepped away from the window, smiling to herself,

and returned to the kids section of the gym. She had one more class to teach, and then she was free for the rest of the day.

Her first stop would be the only one that mattered.

An hour later, showered and moderately put together, Mara got into her car, wishing she'd thought to bring something more appealing than jeans and a sweater to wear. But she had only planned on going back to the bakery to help with the St. Patrick's Day treats for the new promo photos, so comfortable would be more important than fashionable.

If she made it to the bakery at all today, she would be grateful she had chosen this ensemble.

But that was a very big if.

Her family had been remarkably quiet about her separation from Zane, not asking any questions or, seemingly, expecting any explanation. But when Mara had told her mom she wouldn't be over to the bakery until later, that she needed to see Zane first, the response had told her all she needed to know.

*Good.*

So there was that.

Mara shook her head as she drove towards Zane's house. She couldn't even have music on in the car, she was so nervous. How could something that felt so right give her this much anxiety? It just wasn't fair.

"It's your own fault," she reminded herself, gulping down a lump as she pulled into the neighborhood. "You're the one who decided on this break."

She exhaled slowly as she passed the few houses before his, then slowed when the familiar exterior of his place came into view. Her heart shot into her throat, pounding there with a fury that made her slightly nauseated. After pulling in front of the house, she put the car in park and turned off the ignition, shoving her door open before she could think too much about what she was doing. She had done way too much thinking already.

"Can I help you?"

Mara jumped and whirled to her left, one hand flying to her chest.

A middle-aged man with a thick, muscular build stood in the neighbor's driveway, staring at her intently, his smile polite but also intimidating.

Oh boy.

"I'm . . ." She swallowed hastily. "I'm here to see Zane."

"Uh-huh." His smile flicked just a little, his hands slowly going to his hips. "And you are?"

Crap. What was her name?

It clicked suddenly that Zane had told her his neighbor was a cop, and everything slid into place.

"Mara," she told the neighbor, trying for a smile. "Mara Matthews. I'm . . . a friend of the family."

The neighbor chuckled, and his stance eased, though Mara's tension didn't. "I know a little about you, Mara Matthews, but we'll call you a friend of the family for now. I'm Steve." He waved, this time much more friendly. "Zane isn't home right now. They're still out getting pancakes."

Mara hissed under her breath and looked at the house with a wince. "Great. Waiting. It just had to get worse."

"Sorry for the interrogation," Steve went on, oblivious to Mara's current state of mind. "Ever since Chicago, I've taken to being a little more protective."

A flinch screeched across Mara's face, and she looked back at Steve reluctantly. "Really?"

Steve shrugged. "Zane hasn't asked me to or anything, but I take an interest. That little girl is something special, and her daddy does his best for her. I may offer my services as a security detail if he has another event, but that might be too much."

245

Mara had to smile at that, and she folded her arms, moving in his direction. "Maybe, but you never know." She sighed and looked back at Zane's house. "Any idea when they might be back?"

"Well, I can't be positive," Steve drawled, scratching at his chin, "but that right there could be Zane's car pulling into the neighborhood now."

Mara whirled, gasping and half choking on a swallow while her eyes frantically scanned the street. Sure enough, Zane's dark SUV was heading in their direction. And there was no time to move her car or run or make a second attempt at an entrance. She just had to stand here.

Waiting.

She tried for another swallow, but it, too, got caught in her throat.

Her legs shook with the urge to run, and it was all she could do to lock her knees. She would not run from this. From him.

From them.

She took two steps back as his car pulled into the driveway, but her eyes found Zane and refused to look anywhere else.

His eyes seemed intent on doing the same.

He parked the car in the driveway, a good distance from the garage, and sat in his seat while the other doors opened. Just staring at Mara.

"Come on, Hopey-Dope," Josie's voice came from the other side of the vehicle. "Last one inside is a lima bean!"

Car doors slammed, and Mara saw in her peripheral vision Hope and Josie racing towards the house in a flurry of legs, neither saying a word to her.

Mara swallowed, her entire being focused on and attuned to Zane. Zane, who still sat in his car. Zane, who still stared at her.

Zane, who inhaled, exhaled, opened his door, and stepped out.

"Hey, Zane," Steve called out, his voice dropping with laughter.

Zane closed the door of his car and leaned his back against it, eyes on Mara. "Steve."

Mara could hear laughter behind her as Steve walked back up the drive to his house, and then she felt her lungs heave on a relieved breath of air.

They were alone.

"Hi," Mara said softly, the word sounding lame but making her eyes burn all the same.

Zane didn't move. "Hi."

She didn't know how to take that, how to respond to that, and she forced her knees to unlock, if only to keep from passing out on the cement in front of him.

"You're here." His voice wasn't quite flat, but the intonation was unreadable. Not happy, not mad, and not giving anything away.

Mara nodded. "I'm here."

"What does that mean?" He slid his hands into his pockets, which did nothing to ease the tension in his frame. "I'm afraid to ask, quite frankly. I've been climbing the walls for a week, and this ..." He shrugged, the thought going unfinished.

"I'm sorry," Mara whispered, her voice breaking. "Not for what I did, but for how it hurt you. I stand by it, and you have to know why."

To her surprise, he nodded back. "Yeah. Took me a few days, but I got it. You were right. Hope and I come with a full carousel of baggage, and I don't want anyone significantly in our lives who isn't sure they're going to stay there. I don't think I would have been able to handle it if ... well, you know." His mouth finally lifted in a small, crooked smile. "Thanks for being smarter than me here."

She managed a weak smile back. "Smart didn't make it any easier. You do everything in life the way you play hockey, Zane. All heart, all energy, everything you have at all times. It's a beautiful, amazing part of you, maybe the part I love best, and I just . . ." She swallowed once. "I wanted to be able to do the same for you. I had to make sure that you wouldn't have someone else in your life who changed her mind about being there. I didn't want you to be hurt again."

Zane straightened up. "You aren't Michelle, Mara. You never could be."

"I know, but when it comes down to it, she left you both. She wasn't ready." Feeling something strong and warm spreading through her spine, she lifted her chin, her smile growing. "I needed to know if I was ready."

Zane stilled, his chest barely moving, his eyes more intense than she had ever seen them. "And?"

Mara exhaled softly and took a step towards him. "I'm here."

He didn't move except for his eyes, which lowered to her feet and traced the entire length of her up, bringing a blush into her cheeks when his gaze returned to hers. "You understand what this means, right? You cross that distance between us, there's no going back."

She tilted her head, eyes narrowing a little as a ticklish excitement began to settle in. "But you want me to cross it, right?"

Zane exhaled a rough laugh, taking his hat off and running his hands through his hair. "I'm barely hanging on, honestly. But I'm going to." He sobered and dropped his hat, pushing away from his car just a little. "This is your call. You just have to understand: you make it over here, and I'm not letting you go. Ever. That's what we're talking about here. I love you. That's only become more real to me in the last week. It's a lot to ask, and it's really early in this relationship, but those are the stakes for me. All in or nothing at all."

Mara stared at him, the weight of this moment not lost on her. Her heart pounded furiously, but not with fear, nerves, or doubt.

It was love. Soaring, sweeping, ridiculously overwhelming love.

This was it.

She crossed over to him with confident steps and stopped directly before him, looking him dead in the eye. "In," she said firmly, leaving no doubt.

Zane exhaled heavily in relief. "Good." He took her face in his hands and crushed his lips to hers, nothing tentative or hesitant in their attentions. His kisses were both ferocious and fearless, lingering enough to make her tingle, teasing enough to make her squirm, but each and every one wrung pleasure from her in a way that only he could do. That only he had ever done.

She arched into him, pulling herself closer, and he cradled her there, his fingers clutching against her sweater, telling her far more than his words might have. Again and again his mouth took hers, again and again she took his, and when her arms twined tightly around his neck, his hold increased. When she sighed into him, he smiled against her lips. When their lips faintly parted, he simply held her in his arms without speaking, breathing with her until their heartbeats settled into the same steady rhythm.

"I love you," Mara whispered against him, not particularly caring if the words were audible or intelligible.

But he heard them, and he turned his head so his lips could sear the edge of her ear as he said, "I love you too.

Cinnamon speckled, rosy cheeked, sweat drenched, and all. Flame is always on here, Mara. Always."

A sob welled up within her, and Mara pulled back to smile through her tears at him, one hand brushing through his hair. "Here too. I'm Team Zamboni, baby. You've got me for life."

His grin sparked a new fire in her toes, and she curled into him. "Forever teammate? My volleyball buddy Brady will be so disappointed."

Mara burst into laughter and kissed Zane quickly. "Brady can deal. You are *mine*, Zane Winchester. And I'm not sharing."

"You're so competitive," he chuckled as he brushed his nose against hers. "It's ridiculously hot."

"Welcome to Team Z," she shot back. "We take no prisoners."

Zane scooped her up, wrapping her legs around him as he carried her towards the house. "Damn straight, babe. All in, whole game, everything you've got."

Mara touched her brow to his, grinning even as she sighed. "Put me in the game, Coach."

"You're already there, my love. And you're killing it."

He kissed her again, and the crowd went wild.

# EPILOGUE

"Slashing. Two minutes."

"Now you call it?" Zane bellowed in disgust. "Sherman's been pulling that stunt all night, and *now* you call it? Come on, Coop..."

The ref had zero sympathy for Zane's complaint and only gestured for the penalty box.

Zane skated backwards towards the box, shaking his head. "Unbelievable, man. How much are they paying you?"

"Get over there," Coop ordered with a warning look.

Zane mimicked a curtsey and turned around, heading for his box, but not without style. He cupped his hands around his mouth and booed loudly, which the crowd immediately picked up and sent echoing around the arena. He gestured for them to bring up the volume, and they delivered beautifully.

He grinned at them and gave them an appreciative round of applause, making those nearest him laugh.

It was a good night.

Aside from this call.

Even then, it wasn't that bad.

The Hounds were on a roll this year, undefeated so far,

and early predictions had them challenging for the playoffs, if not the cup itself.

Jax and the Flyers would have something to say about that next week, but Zane and his team weren't worried. In fact, they were looking forward to it. They'd come close to beating them last season, and close wasn't acceptable now.

Tonight's game would be good for them, especially if the score stayed put. It was also more of a fun game than anything else, if for no other reason than because it was Declan's team. Normally the two of them didn't have much interaction on the ice, both being defensemen, but Zane had delivered a little gift the period before, and they hadn't shared the ice since.

If the expression on Declan's face right now was any indication, Zane would be in for it when he got out of the box.

That was Declan, though. Hot or cold, never in between, which was where his nickname had come. Just roll the dice and see what you get.

Zane grinned as he saw Declan watching him, and he blew him a kiss for good measure.

Dice just shook his head.

This was going to be beautiful.

Music blared through the speakers while the refs conferred on something or other, the players on the ice waiting to reset for a faceoff. Zane smirked and looked up at the jumbotron, laughing to himself at the antics of the fans when captured on camera.

A sign appeared on the screen then.

*HEY ZAMBONI*

A slow grin crossed his lips at seeing it. He knew that handwriting anywhere, and his heart skipped a beat in anticipation. His wife did this every now and then, holding up a sign to send him a message. Last month she'd turned over a sign with the message *YOU'RE HOT* on the back.

# CROSSCHECK

Things had been very entertaining when he'd gotten home that night.

What would tonight's message from Mara be?

The sign turned over.

*YES!*

Yes? Yes what?

He blinked at the sign, his eyes lowering just enough to see Mara's face beneath it, and her wide, giggling grin caught him like a punch to the gut. Hope was jumping up and down beside her, clearly ecstatic.

Yes?

His jaw dropped as the wheels spun in his mind. That morning's predawn conversation flashed back through his mind at double speed. Mara lying beside him in bed, intertwining their fingers and whispering, "I might be pregnant."

He'd rolled on top of her for a quick interrogation, grinning wildly, and kissed her hard when she'd told him her suspicion again. She'd said she would be taking a test later, and somehow he'd forgotten that in game prep. Completely forgotten.

Until now.

*Yes.*

He shot to his feet with a loud whoop, pumping his fists in the air. "YES!" he bellowed, turning to try and find his family in the stands from his box. The sign caught his attention, and he pointed with both hands at it. "Yes! Yes! Yes!"

The crowd around him was completely lost but cheered with him anyway. He didn't care; he didn't even care that the faceoff was happening and that he should be focusing on the game. Had no idea how much time was left on the powerplay.

He just wanted to climb the plexiglass walls and get to his wife.

They were having a baby.

*YES.*

No one in the arena would know for sure what that was, given the lack of context. Some of them would know he was married, given the nature of the internet and photos from public events, and there was some idea that they had a kid, but they didn't know much else. He and Mara had decided not to prevent publicity about themselves, but they weren't going to encourage it either.

No one in the public knew that Mara had adopted Hope the same day she'd married Zane.

No one knew anything about his life before Mara.

What little life there had been before Mara.

He grinned at her now, though he could barely make her out in the crowd. His chest could have burst with the joy and love and excitement now pumping through him with every beat of his heart.

What the hell was he doing here? He needed to kiss his wife senseless right now, not jump around like an idiot in this box.

"You're good, Zamboni."

Zane turned and looked at the official in the box. He was what?

The official raised a brow and pointed at the ice.

Zane followed his finger.

Oh. Game.

Right.

He shook his head and skated out into the ice, trying and failing to get his head back into the game or figure out where he should be going and what was happening.

He delivered a quick hit to a guy in his way, laughing almost merrily as he did so. The puck suddenly came to him, and he gleefully dribbled it up the ice along the boards.

"Heads up!" someone called from behind him.

Zane looked up just in time to see Dice making a beeline for him, and he shot the puck off to his left before being knocked almost completely off his feet, his head slamming into the boards.

"Wow," he gasped, still laughing as he struggled to right himself.

Dice creamed him again, grabbing his jersey and knocking Zane's stick out of his hands. "Come on. Let's go."

Zane shrugged, grinning. "Okay."

He grunted as Dice landed a hard jab into his cheek, the crowd roaring behind them both. "So I guess this means you're on fire tonight?"

Dice growled. "This is payback. That hit was a target, and you know it."

"Of course it was," Zane replied, still smiling. "It's how I show affection." He slammed a right hook into Dice's face, the skin breaking just enough to draw a little blood. "Feel better?" He threw his head back on a laugh.

"Why are you smiling?" Dice spat blood, gripping the neckline of Zane's jersey. "Your face is going to break, and it's scary." He tried to jab again, but Zane dodged it.

"You see the sign a minute ago?"

Dice stopped fighting but still held onto Zane. "Yeah. What does yes mean? Mara agree to go to prom with you or something?"

Zane let his grin reach its full measure. "Yes means we're having a baby."

Dice's eyes widened, and his mouth fell open. "What?"

"She said yes," Zane laughed, shaking Dice by his jersey with his enthusiasm.

"YES!" Dice whooped and threw his arms around Zane as much as he could, thumping his back hard. "Yes, Z! That's fantastic!"

Zane had no response except to keep laughing.

"Break it up, guys," Coop told them, sounding completely lost as he tried to get his hands between them.

They ignored him and turned to face Mara and Hope, both laughing now as they pointed up at her in victory.

Zane could see Mara more clearly now, and she was shaking her head in the same resigned way she always did when the Pit got up to something.

But she loved them as much as he did, and dinner with Dice tonight would be entertaining.

"Hey, she brought Hope!" Dice remarked as he held out a fist as though to bump hers across the stands.

"Uncle Dec will have some explaining to do later."

Dice shrugged. "Eh, I'll buy her a milkshake tonight."

Zane raised a brow. "Mara or Hope?"

"Shut up." Dice laughed and cuffed him on the back of the head before heading to the penalty box, wiping his cheek free of blood.

Zane looked at Mara again and pointed to the team tunnel. She nodded and got up with Hope while he returned his attention to the last few minutes of the period.

It felt like ages, but when the buzzer sounded, he raced over to the tunnel before any of his teammates.

Mara was waiting for him in the first row of seats, leaning across the barrier as much as she could, laughing and tucking a strand of her dark hair behind her ear.

Zane grabbed a chair from the usher and moved it over to her, climbing on the seat to be able to reach her. "Yes, baby!"

She took his face in her hands, her thumbs sliding over his cheeks. "You're an idiot, Zane. And you're bleeding."

"Baby, we're having a baby!" He laughed and reached up to slide a hand behind her head, pulling her to him for a sound kiss.

She kissed him back, her lips telling him just how she really felt at the moment, and it wasn't irritated or exasperated.

"I love you," she whispered against his lips, kissing him softly again.

"Love you more, hon." He winked and turned his attention to his daughter, who was practically dancing where she stood. "Ready for this, Hopey-Dope?"

She giggled and jumped up and down. "Yes!" Then she frowned. "Why did Uncle Dec hit you?"

Zane chuckled and gave her a high-five. "Ask him at dinner, okay?" He looked back at his wife, shaking his head in disbelief. "I love you so much, Mara. This is amazing, I'm thrilled."

"I can tell." She laughed again and leaned closer, her blue eyes locked on his, stealing his breath, as usual. "Baby Z already has the best daddy in the world. I love you, and I can't wait, Zane. End this game, and let's celebrate."

He pressed close and kissed her hard. "Yes, ma'am. I'll bring the cinnamon rolls."

Mara's cheeks flamed, and she slapped his shoulder, unable to hide a smile as he stepped down from the chair. He laughed, blew his girls a kiss, and headed into the locker room with his bewildered teammates.

"Come on, boys," he said, tossing an arm around Boomer's shoulders. "Let's put this thing away. I've got better plans tonight."

**Rebecca Connolly** writes romances, both period and contemporary, because she absolutely loves a good love story. She has been creating stories since childhood, and there are home videos to prove it! She started writing them down in elementary school and has never looked back. She currently lives in Indiana, spends every spare moment away from her day job absorbed in her writing, and is a hot cocoa addict.

Visit her online: RebeccaConnolly.com

www.ingramcontent.com/pod-product-compliance
Lightning Source LLC
LaVergne TN
LVHW021805060526
838201LV00058B/3240